Reading Allowed

True Stories and Curious Incidents from a
Provincial Library

Chris Paling

CONSTABLE • LONDON

Some names and details have been changed to protect the privacy of others.

CONSTABLE

First published in Great Britain in 2017 by Constable
This paperback edition published in 2018 by Constable

1 3 5 7 9 10 8 6 4 2

A CIP catalogue record for this book
is available from the British Library.

ISBN: 978-1-47212-472-2

Typeset in Sabon by SX Composing DTP, Rayleigh, Essex
Printed and bound in Great Britain by CPI Group (UK) Ltd, Croydon CR0 4YY

Papers used by Constable are from well-managed forests
and other responsible sources.

Constable
An imprint of
Little, Brown Book Group
Carmelite House
50 Victoria Embankment
London EC4Y 0DZ

An Hachette UK Company
www.hachette.co.uk

www.littlebrown.co.uk

For Luca

This is a work of nonfiction. The events are all true but the names and some of the characteristics have been changed.

'We are the only species on the planet, so far as we know, to have invented a communal memory stored neither in our genes nor in our brains. The warehouse of this memory is called the library.'

Carl Sagan

'In common with librarians the world over, the two women were used to a disproportionate number of people acting strangely.'

José Latour

Contents

SUMMER

French Women Don't
Get Facelifts

The Saturday afternoon peace of 'Fiction' is shattered by the arrival of Norris and his mother, Mrs Stone. As they enter the demure and largely silent room Mrs Stone is shouting at Norris at the top of her voice and Norris is shouting back at the top of his. They are not engaged in a heated argument – this is the volume at which they communicate. Mrs Stone is profoundly deaf, Norris is not, but is so conditioned to shouting at his mother that he communicates with the rest of the world at the same volume.

I am new to this library and have not yet encountered the Stones and only too late do I realise that the staff at the other service points have immediately become embroiled in answering complicated queries or have scurried off to shelve the returns. Norris, seeing I am free, makes a beeline for me. He is dressed in a fully buttoned duffel coat. His hair is black, greasy and side parted. He is a tall, lean man in his late thirties or early forties, his eyes are glassy in circular dark sockets and stare unblinking at the world in an expression that hovers somewhere between indignation and incredulity.

'Hello,' I say. 'How can I help you?' I have pitched my voice low in the hope that Norris does the same. He doesn't.

3

'I'd like this,' he shouts and proffers a damp, week-old copy of the *Metro*. I take it from him. It is open on a page plugging a new book about the heart-warming camaraderie between a battlefront soldier and his dog. 'Have you got it?' Norris hollers. 'It looks very interesting. Yeeeesss.'

'I'll check,' I say.

'Yes,' shouts Norris. 'It looks very interesting.'

I begin to enter the enquiry into the system.

'Have you got it?'

'I'm just checking.'

'Yes.'

Norris watches and waits. I feel the weight of his interest. Thankfully the title of the book doesn't throw up the usual three thousand or so search results, but limits itself to three. The heart-warming story is number one and there is a copy available in a library on the other side of the city.

'I can get it,' I tell Norris. 'But it will take a few days.'

'How many days?'

'Difficult to say. Around a week, I should think.'

'How many days?'

'About seven. Shall I reserve it for you?'

'Yes,' shouts Norris. 'It looks very interesting.'

I take Norris' card and make the reservation.

'How many days?' Norris demands for the third time.

'About seven.'

'Yeeeesss . . .' The 'yes' is a dying sigh.

I hand Norris back his library card: 'All done.'

'Yes,' says Norris. 'You can keep the magazine. I don't need it.'

'Thank you.'

Norris waits, continuing to stare at me.

'Can I do anything else?' I ask him.

Without answering, Norris turns smartly and wanders off towards the heart of Fiction, his absence from the desk revealing the sight of his mother who is now shuffling my way. It would be hard to hazard an age for Mrs Stone – perhaps somewhere around seventy. She is small – under five feet tall – and stooped and resembles both in sight and odour a compost heap over which a tarpaulin has been thrown. The higher reaches of the tarpaulin are covered in a white powder of what could possibly be snow but is actually dandruff, and as she gets closer I can see that scattered in the field of dandruff are a number of what look like microscopic hay bales – the haven, perhaps, of tiny hibernating creatures. Mrs Stone is more vegetable than animal, red-cheeked, grey-haired and yellow-toothed and is carrying two enormous canvas bags which, with a weary sigh, she drops on the floor beside my lectern.

'Did he give you the books?' she shouts towards the floor (the direction of all of her subsequent statements and demands).

'The books?'

'Him.' She points a dirt-grained finger towards Norris, who is now standing close to the lift, seemingly trying to stare it out.

'I had one on depression, one on IBS. I like health books.'

'No, he didn't give me any books.'

'What?' She cups her tiny ear with a grubby hand.

'He didn't give me any books,' I say a little louder.

'No books?'

'No.'

'Well, where are they?'

'I don't know. On the trolley?'

'What?'

'They might be on the trolley.' I enunciate more clearly, pointing in the direction of the returns trolley.

'He's a pest.' Mrs Stone casts a malevolent look towards her son. 'Everybody says so. They say so up there.'

'I'll check for you,' I tell Mrs Stone and spend the next five minutes hunting down the six books on her account that she claims Norris has handed in. I find 'Depression' on the returns trolley but there is no sign of the others.

Mrs Stone is unhappy with the result of my search and suggests I look elsewhere. I promise her that I will when she has gone.

'I'll sort it out,' I tell her.

'What! Sort what?'

'Sort out the returns. Don't worry.'

At this point Norris strides over and hands his mother a canvas bag containing six heavy books. One is an encyclopaedia on the history of pop music, three are about steam engines and two are about trolley buses.

'I want these,' he demands. 'I'm going home.' And with that, Norris strides rapidly out of the library. Mrs Stone reaches down, picks up the heavy bag and looks inside.

'He's just had these,' she shouts.

'He's bringing them back?'

'No, he wants them.'

'So you want me to issue them?'

'What?'

'You want me to . . .?'

'I don't know why he wants them. He's just had them.'

The discussion continues for three or four minutes. I issue the books and put them back into Norris' bag. We then turn to Mrs Stone's request.

'I want the other of these,' she shouts and hands over her torn and damp library paperback copy of *French Women Don't Get Facelifts: Aging with Attitude*.

'The other one,' she elucidates.

The book and its French author are unfamiliar to me, but I discover from the system that Mireille Guiliano has written a number of other books. I offer the options to Mrs Stone: 'Which would you like me to reserve? *French Women Don't Get Fat* or *How to Be Chic and Elegant*?'

'Fat? What?'

I repeat the options. Mrs Stone opts for *French Women Don't Get Fat: The Secret of Eating for Pleasure*.

'All done,' I tell her, handing her card back, but she has now lost her purse among the chaos of the belongings strewn around the floor.

'I don't know why you don't have chairs,' she shouts.

In a recent layout change the service desks were replaced by lectern-height service points, presumably to discourage customers from sitting down and chatting too long to the staff.

'I'll get you one,' I say, and fetch a chair for her from beside Brewer, a sleeping rough sleeper, who has been taking refuge in the warm since the library opened.

Mrs Stone receives the chair without thanks, slumps down and begins poking into the foul-smelling recesses of her bags. Finally, she retrieves a light blue tourist's bum bag, which she unzips and puts her card into. She returns the bum bag to one of her other bags and then, for thirty or forty seconds, sits looking at her baggage, mentally preparing herself for the journey ahead.

She stands.

'Thank you,' she says, drawing in a deep breath.

Mrs Stone then somehow manages to transport the three heavy bags out of the library. The compost heap odour lingers for the remainder of the afternoon.

When I change desks half an hour later I find a pile of books

Norris has returned (none of his mother's are among them). They are all tagged and destined for a library on the other side of the city – and are all exact duplicates of the books he has found on the shelves of this library this afternoon. Mrs Stone was right.

When the library closes half an hour later I set off for home on my Vespa. Close to the town hall I see the familiar figure of Mrs Stone. She is trying to mount a tricycle around which are garlanded her three huge bags. Norris is nowhere to be seen.

The Lost Badonger

The first shifts at the central library begin at 8.30 a.m. The large, modern building with its huge loading bay is the hub of all of the libraries in the area, processing the stock to and from the branch libraries and beyond to the UK network. The stock, shared between the central and branch libraries, comprises around half a million books.

I've been here for over two years now and joined after leaving the BBC, where I'd worked as a radio producer with a parallel career as a novelist. I sweated over the first application form I'd written in twenty years and was called for interview. After being shown up to the mezzanine floor of the central library by a senior library manager I was introduced to two shelves of unsorted books and, as an ice-breaker, given five minutes to put them into alphabetical order. An easy starter you'd imagine. It wasn't. I began confidently but was then stalled by questioning whether the Mcs come before the Macs. The next tricky one was whether Conan Doyle is shelved with the Cs or the Ds? And what about Eric Van Lustbader – V or L? Daphne du Maurier – D or M? And what about the nonfiction Dewey system with its three digits followed by several decimal qualifiers? Somehow I made enough sense in front of the interview panel to be invited to join the team though I sweated over the 'How do you respond to a customer who swears they've returned a book but it's still on their card and there's no evidence of it on the shelves?' After a brief period as a fully fledged 'library officer', I eventually settled for the more flexible life of a 'casual' – the same job but on a zero-hours contract. This enabled me to maintain the pretence that on my days off I would continue writing the next novel.

The first tasks of those on the early shift at the central library are to set up the upper and lower floors, put out the newspapers and open the 'Van Boxes'. These are hefty green crates delivered by a grey-faced, cadaverous man in a Transit van. In another life he would have been the collector of corpses for a funeral director. The crates contain various items of post and books in transit from the community libraries. The boxes are trolleyed down to the main floor in the lift and stacked in high columns beside the automatic issues/returns machines (the 'RFID' machines) and whoever has been allocated the task begins the process of discharging the books inside them; distributing them to the reserves shelf or back to the returns shelving depending on what the machine has told them to do. Soon the jolt of morning caffeine enlivens the early workers into conversation. Somebody asks: 'Any news on the badonger?' Nobody has heard anything. It's agreed that the issue should be raised at the 9.45 briefing, the consensus being that we can't operate efficiently with only two badongers on the ground floor.

Over the next half hour, the PCs are turned on, the newspapers are stamped and put out, yesterday's collected and reassembled, any over a week old are crammed into the recycling bin. The counter stock of joining cards and leaflets is refilled, the paper supplies in the printers and photocopiers checked, the 'expired reserves' (anything over a month old) are returned to the stock, the tills are filled, the walkie-talkies distributed and switched on to channel 16, the Silver Bin (the overnight drop-box) is emptied with caution – you never quite know what you'll find in there – while the cleaners vacuum the floors, wipe down the tables, chip off the hardened unidentifiable residues from the floor of Children's and mop the lino. If there's an exhibition being set up then 'Facilities' will be on hand to advise the people who have hired the space, explaining to the exhibitors that it's unwise to trail thin electric cables across access corridors. Facilities facilitate almost everything in the library that the library officers don't – they act as security guards, photocopier repairers, shelf movers, lost-property administrators, door lockers, bouncers, secret police, maintenance staff and toilet unblockers. They have seen it all – many times.

In the café, the barista dons a new apron, slides up the metal roller blind in front of the chiller cabinet and grinds a fresh batch of coffee beans. She pushes a switch and the midget refinery of her Italian espresso machine lights up. Conference attendees arrive with their bought-in cappuccinos and shoulder bags and are directed to the appropriate room on the mezzanine where their colleagues await them among the urns and sugary pastries. Slowly the production line of information grinds into operation. Somebody usually puts on a CD in the Large Print section (formerly the CD/DVD area, hence the CD player) which provides a soundtrack to the early labours of the day. Today it's *The Velvet Underground & Nico* and Lou Reed's hungover drawl suits the mood of the morning well.

At 9.45 the tannoy announces a call to the daily staff briefing, which takes place at the main desk. The staff arrive from all corners of the building and gather in a semi-circle around the duty managers. Some lean on shelves, others wheel up chairs from the PCs. Some listen intently, some scoff, some chat between themselves, and some dream. Today it's announced that two customers have received banning orders, the details of which are in envelopes left for them behind the counter. It's suggested that should one of these customers come in, the member of staff at the main desk can either hand over the envelope or radio for a manager. One has been banned for violent conduct so we should be wary. The printer situation is reported on (today, the public printers are working) and the rota is handed out.

The library operates a shift system of hourly change (recently changed to two-hourly). This provides variety to the day and ensures that nobody is detained for too long on the busiest stations or in the ear-splitting Children's area. The final issue on the briefing agenda is an announcement that there are problems with the sewer: it's reported that the public toilets have been heard to be 'gurgling' and we should keep an eye out (and presumably an ear and a nose) for the situation worsening. All of the updates are in the 'Day Book' which, as its name suggests, is a diary listing all of the events and updates for each day plus the numbers of those who have attended events in the library.

'Anything else?' the manager asks.

A hand goes up: 'Any news on the badonger?'

'Not yet.'

'Only we're a bit short on the ground floor.'

'We've ordered one but it hasn't come.'

The 'badonger' is a heavy, palm-sized, circular lump of shiny metal with a half-inch groove cut down the centre. It's the device used to release the security tags on the CD cases, allowing the CDs to be slid out of the case and issued. There were three on the ground floor – one at each workstation – but one has recently been stolen. Anything not literally screwed down is fair game for some of the regular users of the library.

No more hands are raised so the meeting is dismissed and the staff move to their posts to log in to the two computer systems – the stock circulation programme and 'Netloan', which administers the public's PC bookings across all of the libraries in the group. The download button is pressed and yesterday's logs of loans and returns are dumped down the line. After a moment or two of silence and peace, Trev, or one of the other Facilities team, calls a warning: 'Opening the doors, all you lovely people!' and, after a brief pause, the day begins as thirty or forty people surge in like a crowd at a Harrods' sale (in the exam periods students literally run for the stairs, making for the PCs or the quietest study desks upstairs in Nonfiction, or, in the case of the street sleepers, the toilets).

Stalled at Alexandria

An effete, shaven-headed man in a well-cut suit of shiny cloth is loudly and angrily discussing his new shrink on his mobile phone. He is pacing the narrow corridor in the far reaches of Nonfiction.

'. . . He was simply a name given to me. I don't know anything about his credentials so . . . he still didn't tell me. Well, I'm sorry . . . well, well, maybe a bit as I said to him I don't choose a dentist without knowing about his training. When I buy something I like to know what I'm buying. Maybe he trained at a place which has a terrible reputation. I'm entitled to know. How else can I assess? . . . I . . . I . . . Maybe he's a fake. How do I know, you know? Really it was making me very angry. I nearly walked out. Yes, that's not about my problems, it's about . . . It's my right. He didn't even give me a card . . . yeah, he's . . . but that doesn't say anything. So . . . that irritates me. Yes, I nearly got up and walked out. I've got to take a call. All right, sweetie, goodbye . . .' (No call taken.)

I return to the book I'm preparing to shelve. The cover catches my eye. It's too enticing to slide it immediately into its place. You will often come across librarians stalled beside a shelf having been trapped by a cover or the blurb on a book. The title of this one demands that it be opened. It's Alberto Manguel's *The Library at Night*, a series of essays on libraries as 'myth', 'order', 'space', 'power', 'shadow', etc. Manguel, the inside cover suggests, is an Argentinian/Canadian novelist, translator, anthologist and essayist. It's quiet today so I lean against the stack and begin to read. From the vantage point of his own extensive library in a fifteenth-century barn on a hill south of the Loire, Manguel ruminates on the universe, its 'dearth of meaning and discernible purpose'. To counter this, to lend the world a semblance of sense and order, he suggests we have collected 'whatever scraps of information we can gather in scrolls and books and computer chips, on shelf after library shelf'. He explains that the Library of Alexandria set the pattern for what we have today. It 'rose when stories took on the shape of books, and strove to find a syntax that would lend each word, each tablet, each scroll its illuminating and necessary place. Indistinct, majestic, ever-present, the tacit architecture of that infinite Library continues to haunt our dreams of universal order.'[1]

The Library of Alexandria was a learning centre established by the Ptolemaic kings at the end of the third century to follow the teachings of Aristotle. Until the founding of Alexandria the libraries of the ancient world were either private collections or government storehouses where legal and literary documents were kept for official reference. Manguel explains, 'The Library of Alexandra revealed a new imagination that outdid all existing libraries in ambition and scope.' The kings of Pergamum in north-west Asia Minor tried to compete with Alexandria and build a library of their own, but, 'To prevent their rivals from creating manuscripts for their library, the Ptolemies banned the exportation of Papyrus, to which the Pergamum librarians responded by inventing a new writing material which was given the city's name: *pergamenon*, or parchment.'[2]

My reading is interrupted by: 'Do you work here?'

'I'm sorry?'

'Ah – are you a member of staff?'

'Yes.'

It's an elderly man in a cap. 'I'm afraid the lavatory is blocked.'

'Ah. Thank you.'

I bid goodbye to Alexandria but, before reporting the blockage to Facilities on the walkie-talkie, I return to the desk and issue the book to myself.

Children's

The apostrophe slung around the end of 'Children's' destabilises the word and leaves the description hanging there, waiting for completion – Children's what? It is, of course, the children's section of the library, an area one would fondly imagine to be a haven for classic books (*Swallows and Amazons*, *The Lion, the Witch and the Wardrobe*, Harry Potter, etc.) and a few improving DVDs. One might also picture a tidy, well-mannered parade of largely middle-class men and women carefully shepherding their indulged offspring towards the tidy C. S. Lewis or J. K. Rowling sections before returning to the BMW estate with a word of brisk thanks and a genial comment about how wonderful and important libraries are to the community and, were they ever to be threatened, then they'd certainly protest loudly as they would in support of Radio 4 or any of the few other cultural necessities of their world.

The reality is quite different. Children's is a seething, chaotic, noisy souk of colliding infants, breastfeeding mothers, svelte East European au pairs – legs tucked beneath them on the sofas, eating plain yogurt and keeping their hard eyes on their charges – and weary grandparents in sensible coats being tugged towards the DVDs by their pre-school grandchildren. Depending on the time of day the odour of filled nappies also hangs over the area. The room is literally knee-deep in children and the staff in there engage in a battle of attrition with the younger toddlers who tend to teeter along the stacks tugging books off the lowest shelf and dropping them onto the floor. This is usually done with great deliberation but without malice. When walking around Children's it's necessary to keep looking downwards to avoid the dozens of babies and toddlers moving purposefully around the byways of the berserk multi-coloured landscapes that exist in their developing brains.

The atmosphere is calmed by a waterfall of light that cascades down from a long, narrow lightwell in the ceiling illuminating a dark blue wall on which are hung large and colourful ceramic representations of various aquatic creatures. The furniture is comfortable, in primary colours, and, among the low seats and beanbags, are a number of wooden bins containing large picture books. Most of these are usually on the floor, utilised by the six or seven young children sitting on the carpet looking at the books, wearing them, standing on them, carefully dismantling them or having them read by their predominantly female carers. There's also a dressing-up chest and one of the small children has usually donned the popular ladybird costume and is ladybirding around the room, sometimes being pursued by another small child dressed as a wasp.

Today, a young woman in a belted mac and a beret is sitting with her child next to her on one of the low comfortable seats. The child is contentedly leafing through a picture book, which is on her knee. The woman, on her mobile phone, is weeping copiously. A Chinese couple on a bench seat are book-ending their two-year-old and taking it in turns to read about the weather to him. He occasionally stops and points at a picture and they elucidate. A man in tan shorts is wandering around looking for a bin into which he can put his cappuccino cup. His daughter is sitting at one of the computers playing a game. A Japanese couple are at one of the tiny wooden tables with their two young children and eating sushi from cardboard trays. Another woman sits with her young son on her knee. He is facing away from her, a book on his lap. As he silently turns the picture pages I see her surreptitiously smell his hair. Her face remains there, hovering in close proximity to the crown of his head. Another fair-haired toddler is standing beside the wooden oven gleefully opening and closing the door over and over again. And there is a man – Joseph, late twenties – who is always there with his pre-school daughter. He arrives mid-morning almost every day and remains until mid-afternoon. His attention is fixed on his young blonde daughter, who teases him by dashing away and hiding. Occasionally he engages one of the mothers in con-versation – he is the only regular male who visits with his child. I hear snatches of the discussion and I learn from them that his wife is the breadwinner and that she works long days and that he cares for his daughter. It's not uncommon, but he struggles to belong to the tribe. The mothers try to accommodate him in their floor circles and sometimes he joins in, but he's excluded by dint of his sex so usually he makes an excuse to sit apart (though just within earshot) on a low chair, watching his child and waiting for the day to be over.

Today, it's also the weekly 'Story Time' and a young female library officer is reading to fifteen attentive pre-schoolers, all either sitting or lying on the floor like battlefield casualties. She is perching on a low chair and, as she turns each page, she holds it up, turns it, and shows it to her (largely) silent audience before moving on.

As I watch and listen a man approaches my desk followed

by a six-year-old boy in a school uniform (green blazer, grey shorts). The lean man, in his early seventies, has a good head of steel-grey hair, tender eyes and very large oil-grained hands that look like they've been used for manual work: an engineer's hands, not the ruined hands of a career builder. The smell of diesel lingers on his vintage zippered leather flying jacket. He is tentative; apologetic for disturbing me. I reassure him that it's my job to be disturbed by people using the library. He asks if he can take out a book for his grandson on his adult ticket and beckons Jake towards him with a wave of his hand. Jake, a shy boy, approaches the desk with a large book about whales. I explain to the man that he can borrow the book on his ticket but another option would be to make Jake a member. It's a small and unremarkable offer but the man is genuinely taken aback. I have made his day – possibly his week.

'That will earn me brownie points with my daughter,' he says, before asking Jake if he'd like to join. Jake nods. I offer him the choice of two library cards and he opts for the most colourful one. During the joining process the man continually apologises for disturbing me and I repeatedly reassure him that it's my job. Every so often he looks towards his grandson and I see that there's a distance between them that he just can't breach. It's almost as if he wants to reach out and hold him but something – some conditioning – holds him back. Jake, being shy and slightly reserved, won't make the move himself but his eyes convey the fact that he loves his granddad very much.

I present Jake with his new library card. His grandfather prompts him to thank me. He does and I issue him his whales book and then they both leave, on their way to the dentist's, six clear feet of space between them but strongly tied together. Love loses its complications when it leapfrogs a generation.

Summer

I become aware of the blonde top of a small head at the desk. I look over the edge and a three-year-old girl is waiting patiently with a picture book almost half as tall as she is. The book is about bread – the history, how to make it, etc. The girl might have been there for some time but she seems content. Her mother approaches, having left her other child, a babe in arms, being attended to by the grandmother. The woman explains that she'd like to make her daughter a member of the library and I begin the process, the child all the time hugging the book about bread tight to her cardigan in case one of the other children in the library tries to wrest it from her. She's a self-contained, assured child, as yet unaware of the effect of her personality on those around her. When I present her with her library card she puts it carefully into the pocket of her cardigan. Her mother asks her if she'd like to choose a few more books. She declines, explaining to her that the only one she wants is the book on bread and she intends to read it to her brother 'on the settee' that evening. They wander away, back to the grandmother. The girl repeats her intention to her grandmother, who smiles back fondly.

I catch the tail end of a conversation between a woman and her young daughter. They are discussing what the child will eat when they get home: 'Baked beans on toast or gnocchi, Samantha?' the woman asks. Samantha opts for the beans on toast.

Bookmark 1

Various items and scraps of paper (sometimes twigs or dried leaves) are used as bookmarks and left, forgotten, between the pages for the staff to find. Today, in the embrace of *Sons and Lovers*, it's an optimistic young woman's CV.

It begins with this personal statement:

> A hard-working and dedicated individual. Available to work Tuesdays, Wednesdays, Thursdays and the majority of weekends. Cares deeply about the environment and equality. Aims to eventually open a small publishing company as well as becoming a published author, performance poet and university lecturer.

The Sweet Smell of Success

When it was explained to me that the training period for a library officer was two to three weeks I assumed my new boss ('your trousers are your office') was joking. He wasn't. I'd fondly imagined the job to be fairly stress-free, assuming there would be a simple computer programme to master but, beyond that, I envisaged a sedentary occupation that would involve long periods of chatting and no unpleasant situations with which to deal. I'd had quite enough of that in a long career as a radio producer and numerous other short-term jobs at which I'd tried my hand (post-BBC, a brief spell in a pie factory provided me with the worst eleven hours in my employment history).

The complexities of the computer systems aside it took only a day on the shop floor to learn that that the role of a library officer – beyond supplying and receiving books and information – encompasses that of confidant, counsellor and mediator. Mediation is required on most days due to the preponderance of bemused, threatening and often deeply troubled people who use the facilities – many of them rough sleepers. A recent survey found the number sleeping rough in this city has doubled over the past five years. A local waste collection company reported that more than three hundred people had been discovered taking refuge in their hoppers. They have now taken to pasting red stickers on all of them warning that it's inadvisable to sleep in them. A young man who'd missed the last train home did so and it cost him his life.

When the library opens each morning the street dwellers are at the front of the crowd at the door waiting to come in. Wolf, one of the regulars, has a large, crimson, wheeled transatlantic flight-type suitcase which he stores in the gap in the Fiction shelving (between A and B). He then settles himself at one of the computers, taking advantage of his daily free online hour. Wolf is undoubtedly entitled to two free hours, but because he's not receiving benefits he has no proof of the concessionary entitlement. It's unlikely that he features on many databases (I'm not sure if the council's rough-sleepers team have a system), having fallen off the grid many years ago. Every time I have seen him he is wearing a red woollen jumper. His hair is as wild as his thick black beard. Wolf is not a threatening presence, indeed he seems fairly tuned out of the world around him, and between stints on the computer he sits on one of the triangular seats between the shelving units, thin legs drawn up beneath him, chin resting on his knees, watching, but not seeing the people around him. Like most of the street people who come in he seems out of place with a roof over his head, almost as if, by adapting to the savage cold and tough conditions, he has become feral to survive. When at rest he preserves his energy by falling into a state of hibernation.

Despite his unthreatening appearance, like many rough sleepers who lack basic washing facilities, he does smell strongly and, today, a well-dressed, late middle-aged, corpulent man in country casuals (tweed jacket, mustard-coloured cords, highly polished vintage chestnut-brown brogues, silk cravat, tailored shirt) has taken the seat next to him. The man settles but then catches the first whiff of his neighbour. His hand goes to his nose as if he can somehow block it. He then shifts around and looks directly at Wolf, who is oblivious to him. The well-dressed man returns to his screen. A moment later he breaks away and demands: 'Is it necessary for you to come in here and smell up the place?'

Wolf either doesn't hear him or chooses not to reply, but goes on with his browsing.

'Mm?' The man prompts. 'Your clothes, it's . . .' but he can't find the words to describe the smell. His observation tails off with a shake of his head and a loud tut. He resettles himself at the screen.

A pause.

'Do you work?' The man breaks the silence again. 'Have you worked?' Again he is ignored. 'Grief!'

'Lottery,' Wolf says quietly to himself.

'What?'

'Win the lottery.'

The well-dressed man looks at him, stands and walks out in disgust.

The previous night was a stormy one with heavy rain, conditions unconducive to sleeping outdoors. Another of the regulars has fallen asleep, head on the pillow of his arms. He is now snoring loudly. Facilities Trev arrives, stands behind him and wakes him gently by shaking his shoulder. It takes Brewer a moment to orientate himself.

'You know you can't sleep here, friend,' Trev says.

Brewer shakes himself awake and looks around the room. He seems to be seeing it for the first time. Trev troops off, whistling.

The issue of hygiene in libraries exercised the writer Alan Bennett's mother – but her concern lay with the books themselves. In one of his wonderful pieces of reminiscence printed in the

London Review of Books, Bennett wrote, 'I have always been happy in libraries, though without ever being entirely at ease there.'[3] No surprise given that it's hard to envisage anywhere that Bennett would ever feel entirely at ease. But one of his first sanctuaries was Armley Public Library in Leeds, where he paid 2d for a reader's ticket in 1940. His mother, he tells us, was an avid reader when she was younger but 'she always thought of library books as grubby and with a potential for infection – not intellectual infection either. Lurking among the municipally owned pages might be the germs of TB or scarlet fever, so one must never be seen to peer at a library book too closely or lick your finger before turning over, still less read a book in bed.'[4] His mother would have been pleased that nowadays on each service point can be found a dispenser of antiseptic hand cream which the staff use assiduously, especially in the winter-flu season.

The fragrance of Startled Stewart is intrusive in another way. Stewart is a flamboyant gay man of indeterminate age – somewhere between twenty-five and forty. He's a caricature of the kind of gayness depicted by the British film industry of the 1960s. He wears strong aftershave, very white shirts (occasionally smocks), slim-fit slacks, and the shiny skin of his face argues for serious application of skincare products and fake tan, which contrasts the clear brightness of his eyes. His hair is black – too black – so much so that he looks like an American undertaker. He dresses well and is always in a great hurry even though he does not have a regular job ('my nerves'). The library is on one of his rat runs around the city along with his shoe repairer, his GP, his favourite off licence, ethnic clothes shop, charity shops, coffee house, deli and gay bar (he eschews the larger, more modern, clubby establishments, preferring the small, single-roomed Victorian pubs). He pops in regularly for a chat (usually late afternoon) but has never, to my knowledge, borrowed a book. Stewart's other defining characteristic is that he is always unwell.

'I've got another head on me,' he announces as he arrives at the desk. Pinch-clamping his first finger and thumb to his brow, he squints towards the large clock on the wall.

'What's the time?' he asks. 'I can't see a thing. Migraine.'

'Just after four.'

'So . . .' Startled Stewart begins – the prelude to one of his anecdotes. 'I was robbed last night.'

'No.'

'Yes. They took my bag – keys, cards, library card. The lot.' Here he pauses for a short jazz-hands interlude.

'They?'

He pauses. 'Yes . . . them. Two boys. Little devils.' He could be chastising his sons.

'Where were you?'

He names one of the rougher gay bars in the city.

'I should know better, I really should. I've spent all morning running round cancelling my cards. I know who it was. I mean, I do know them but they've apparently gone back up to town.'

I offer more sympathy and suggest he contacts the police. Stewart laughs at the ludicrousness of the suggestion. He looks back at the clock. 'Four?'

'Just after.'

He tuts. 'Must dash.'

Later, a customer reports that the downstairs toilets are blocked. Facilities are radioed – little do they know it but the sewers will be on the agenda for weeks to come.

The Eternal Pieman

A lean male, mid/late twenties, with long sideburns, gelled hair, wearing a standard business suit, is pacing the Crime shelving on his mobile. He has an Essex estuary voice:

'. . . We're going to go away, right? You, me, Gary, Mum, Dad, we're going to go away . . . Yeah, OK, fair enough, I'm not on his back. Yes, fair enough . . . Yes, I . . . OK, I won't speak to him, I won't ask for anything else, don't worry . . . But do you think it's a good idea? . . . Forget the kids, this is just us . . . When are you, when are you, when are you around? Are you definitely around this weekend, Thursday night stroke Friday, can we hook up then? . . . That's cool, we can do that. And then . . . yeah. OK. But I'm with you, all right? Don't worry. Don't worry. Just need to, em, look after, just wanted to ring you and say . . . F*** him . . . Listen, get yourself well and don't worry, right? Don't do it. Don't do it . . . And you, OK? Speak to you later, OK? Bye, sis.'

The man dashes out, looking at his watch. He crosses with one of the regulars, Aaron, on his way in through the automatic sliding doors. If you don't pick up the clues to Aaron's profession when you first meet him (paint-specked lace-up shoes, collarless white shirt, Lucian Freud-type silk scarf worn in lieu of a tie, beanie hat covering his thinning hair), he will offer the information early in the conversation. He is, of course, an art-ist. He's young in outlook and enthusiasms, late middle-aged in years.

His work falls into the *faux naïf* category – huge suns and childlike drawings of animals. I doubt he's sold much, if any, of it. There's a small area close to the entrance to the library that can be hired by the week for a reasonable sum by people wanting to hawk their art. Aaron has used it once. He didn't sell anything but seemed to enjoy his time in the public eye, standing by the main doors of the library and greeting those who came in.

His lack of insight into his shortcomings makes him one of the lucky ones. In his own eyes he is an undiscovered talent and, to him, it's important to be seen living the life of an artist. He served his time at St Martin's (apparently), so he presumably knows the rudiments. He lives in a shared, rented house and when his housemates run out of patience with him not paying his share of the rent, he moves on, sofa-surfing. He's penurious but content. His genius, though, is for sniffing out freebies – usually food. His latest discovery is a café in a deconsecrated church where he can eat a huge lunch and pay literally pennies on the grounds that the users of the scheme pay what they feel the food is worth. The young, idealistic folk who run it are tolerant of him although he falls outside their ideal customer demographic – those in genuine need and distress. I know all of this because Aaron delivers information to you whether you want it or not. He is stuck on transmit.

Today, he's excited. He's returning a huge book on Chinese watercolours and explains that it's given him the glimpse of a new direction his work can take. But his excitement has been triggered by other things. The first is that the local art shop is giving away samples of artist-grade oil paint. The pockets of his brown corduroy jacket are full of them. The staff in the shop know him but, presumably, didn't have time to hide the freebie box before he sprinted to the top of the stairs (art materials are on the first floor) and spotted them. But the main source of his excitement is a pie. It's in a small, cubed cardboard box and bears the logo of a high-end manufacturer.

'Why are you holding up that pie?' I ask him. It's the kind of blunt question you'd probably not ask one of the ordinary customers but I know Aaron.

'It's an everlasting pie.'

'Everlasting?'

'Eternal.'

For once, having dangled a piece of information, he doesn't develop it further.

'Go on then. Tell me why.'

'OK. So . . .' He opens the cardboard box, takes out the pie (beef and stilton) and also removes a small ticket. He holds it up, announcing: 'This ticket allows the bearer another pie. There is, and I checked this at Tesco's, no need to make a further purchase to redeem the free pie, therefore I will now return to the shop and claim another pie. I will leave the shop with said pie, remove the voucher from the box and return to the shop to claim my next free pie. I will continue to do this until the stocks have been fully depleted.'

Aaron dashes out to retrieve his free pie before they run out.

Mid-morning in Nonfiction and the tall windows are framing the bright sunlight rendering the screen of my PC unreadable. A forty-something, large, bearded man approaches the desk. He's tanned and fit and looking for a book on hiking. I take him to the section and leave him to browse. When he returns he seems to want to talk. The main issue on his mind is his daughter, who is in her early teens.

'I'm doing an access course,' he tells me. 'A GCSE in Maths so I can help her. She's a bright kid but she doesn't work so I've signed up at the local college. I hated school. Hated it.'

'In Ireland?' I prompt, alerted by the man's accent.

He goes on. 'Yes.' This is a stepping-stone into reminiscences about his awful time at school: 'I got beaten. We all got beaten by the nuns or the Christian Brothers. Whether you got your work right or wrong they'd beat you. You wouldn't get away with it now, obviously . . .' he shakes his head in disgust. 'One Brother thought he was James Bond. He used to march up and down the aisle in sunglasses with a leather strap and he'd bring it down across your knuckles. Hard. Another one, he took English. He set us homework to write a poem. A hundred lines. So we went to his desk and read our poems out. The first lad, he'd only written about thirty lines, so he pushed him against the wall and beat him across the face. Pretty much all of us got a beating that day . . . Is that the way to teach poetry?'

He goes on to tell me that after school he tried to join the Irish Navy but the processing took too long (he claimed they only had two gunboats, anyway) so he joined the Army instead and went peacekeeping in the Lebanon. He spent his life moving from job to job – Merchant Navy, factory work, going round the world. Although he was brought up in Ireland his roots, he says, are planted deep in the eccentric soil of Cornwall.

'I met my Cornish grandmother only once,' he says. 'I'd come over here as an adult. Not before. She lived in a bungalow at the top of a hill. I remember it clearly. Just the bungalow. On its own. I went with my father's brother, up the hill. He let us in. Didn't knock. We just walked in. The woman was in a chair in the living room. "Is that Bill's son?" she asked my uncle. He told her I was. "Oh," she said. She didn't look in my direction again. That was the only time I met her. She never addressed a single word to me.'

Now he's married and seems to have found a place to settle with his wife and his teenage daughter, who he's trying to help with her Maths.

Five-fingered Discount

Today's staff briefing begins with an update on the book thief.

A woman, late twenties, has been reported stealing goods from the bookstore. She's been caught on CCTV and her mug shot is now up on the walls in case she returns. This has happened before, but this is the first time she's been caught on film in the act.

The rogue's gallery of mug shots on Facilities' small office wall (where the CCTV monitors are housed) is appended with a thumbnail sketch of each of the miscreant's misdemeanours – 'Swearing at staff', 'Threatening violence', 'iPod thief' and, on the newest one, 'Spitting on the carpet'.

The daily printer update is that the machine in Nonfiction is working but the ground-floor one has run out of toner and we're awaiting supplies so all print jobs will be diverted upstairs. Customers are to be directed to the first floor should they want to print anything. This provokes a number of weary looks from the assembled staff. Although redirecting a customer's printing from one floor to another is relatively straightforward, because the IT systems are often breaking down this will inevitably cost time, queues lengthening, customers getting annoyed, and staff having to bear the brunt of the blame for a system over which they have no control.

The morning briefing moves on to the recent layout changes to the library. 'Film' has been moved from a side room to the main floor area. Film is a useful generator of income to the library service. DVDs are rented out for a week, their cost determined by the age of the film. The service has a number of die-hard regulars and is popular among those who come in on a weekly basis with their carers or minders. Their library status being 'fully exempt', DVDs incur no charges. When issues arise there, however, it can embroil the staff member in lengthy negotiations.

The first customer of the day is a young man with his carer. Simon, in his early twenties but with the erratic behaviour of a hyperactive three-year-old, arrives at the desk with two DVDs he is returning – *Annie* and *The Railway Children*.

'Did you enjoy them?' I make the mistake of asking him.

'Rowing boat,' he says.

'Rowing boat?'

He points to the *Railway Children* DVD. 'Blue rowing boat.' He mimes the action of rowing. I ask him if any trains were involved in the film and he tells me that they were not and repeats that this is the story of a blue rowing boat. His carer – a Russell Brand lookalike – tells Simon it's time to choose some more DVDs, but Simon has now decided to run through all the changes that have been made to the layout of the library since he last came in. There has been a major rejigging of the place and a re-siting of a number of sections.

'Stairs there,' he says, pointing to the access to the first floor. 'Stairs. Chairs small. Those shelves. Films here. There.' He points and explains that the film section has been moved, that the café is smaller and various seats have been shifted. His eye for detail is precise and remarkable and he will not be diverted from his task. He has missed nothing. His carer allows him to speak and finally, some five minutes later, there is nothing more to be said and he lets himself be led to the shelves to choose another couple of DVDs. He returns quickly with the cardboard sleeve to the Beatles' animated *Yellow Submarine* DVD. The DVD itself should be in the cupboard behind the counter. It's not there. Nor is it in a couple of other obvious places. As I kneel down for a closer look at the bottom shelf I'm aware of Simon's face about a foot from my own. He begins riffling through the DVDs in the cupboard. I explain that I don't really need his help but he's now looking through the CDs and is oblivious to the ineffectual calls from his carer to return to the public side of the counter. The DVD is nowhere to be found. I apologise to Simon and ask him if he wants to choose another film. I expect some protest but Simon grabs the empty DVD sleeve and runs back to the shelf, returning almost immediately with *A Hard Day's Night*. I issue it and Simon and his carer leave.

I spot Joseph entering (earlier than usual). Today, he's wearing shorts and a T-shirt and, as always, is trailing a few steps behind his daughter, who is dashing down the slope into Children's. Joseph is also wearing his habitual smile and radiates Zen-like calm.

A man, William, in his late twenties, then arrives at the desk already angry. After a few moments in his company I discern that this is his default position; the only movement from it will be for him to become angrier and then, perhaps, violent. He is conventionally dressed in that he doesn't have anything that marks him out as a potentially difficult customer, but, like Norris Stone, his eyes are deeply unsettled and unsettling. Norris' expression allows the possibility that the world will surprise and entertain him, William's does not. Somebody, somewhere down the line, has got it in for him and he is no longer taking it.

He has come to take out six DVDs, all of them American action movies from the Chuck Norris heyday. Having deposited the DVDs on the desk beside the terminal his card is scissored from the top pocket of his denim jacket with the first and second fingers of his right hand and plonked on top of the pile. He looks at the pile and then offers a challenging look towards me. I ask him if he'd like me to issue them.

'What else would you do with them?' he demands.

I manage a thank you and, I think, a reasonable smile and scan his card. On it is an outstanding charge of £36. Anything over £10 automatically blocks the account. I appraise him of the situation. He stares. We wait. He continues to stare. I can only assume he's formulating a response and have no choice but to wait for him to do it. Behind him another man has joined the queue to be served.

'That's not right,' William eventually suggests.

'What's not right?'

'The fines.'

The charges (we're cautious of using the pejorative 'fines' term), I explain to him, are for three DVDs, all of which continue to be overdue – i.e. they are still out and are accruing further fines each day.

'Which ones?' he says.

I list the three DVDs – two American action films and one British gangster movie (*Layer Cake*).

'No,' he says.

'No?'

'I never had them.'

'You didn't take them out?'

'I never had them.'

I check his account and tell him, 'You took them out on June 15th.'

'No.'

Confronted by a customer who claims not to have taken out items, the member of staff has a number of options, the first of which is to suggest the customer is not being entirely truthful. This is a tough judgement call but it can be influenced by information held on the customer's library card. On it there's a category labelled 'claimed returned'; this reveals the history of items the customer has suggested have been returned by them but for some inexplicable reason have not made their way back into the stock. William has nine 'claimed returned' items. He also has a lengthy history of charges. Had the three DVDs been romances his case for not having taken them out would obviously have been stronger. All I can do is repeat that we have, on record, the fact that he has taken out three DVDs in June and they have not been returned. I await his response.

'Why are you looking at me like that?' William says. He is now overtly less angry, but his calmer voice is somehow more chilling.

'Like what?'

'Like that.'

'I'm waiting for you to tell me what you want me to do.'

'I don't like your attitude,' he says.

'I'm sorry,' I tell him, 'but I'm afraid you need to pay the charges and also pay for the lost DVDs.'

'I've told you, I didn't take out the DVDs.'

At this point it's usually wise to call in reinforcements and so I ask a colleague to check William's account to make sure I haven't misread it, misunderstood it or made any assumptions I shouldn't have made. She attests that the DVDs were, indeed, issued to him on 15 June. What weakens William's case is the fact that he's not protesting any more strongly. If, as he claimed, he hadn't taken out the DVDs it's likely that he would be angrier.

'I want to see a manager,' he says. 'I want to make a complaint about you.'

'All right,' I tell him. 'If you'd like to wait over there I'll call a manager down.'

William slumps into a chair beside the desk, stretches out his legs, crosses them at the ankles and stares malevolently at the man in the queue (now four-strong) behind him. I call for a manager on the walkie-talkie and then deal with the waiting customers. This being a library rather than a shop they are less impatient than you'd expect and seem to have quite enjoyed the exchange. Eyebrows are raised in William's direction but I know I have to remain neutral. I tell myself that William, like many of the more testing customers, perhaps has issues that manifest themselves in unsocial behaviour. Maybe William isn't simply a profoundly miserable, sociopathic and angry individual, perhaps some condition dictates the face he presents to the world.

When the manager comes down she begins by checking William's account. William remains slumped in the chair, watching her; watching me. Reluctantly he stands when she calls him to the counter. She explains to him that she has no choice but to repeat what I and my other colleague have already explained to him. It's William's last chance to ratchet up his anger one or two levels to indicate that we are at fault and not him. But he doesn't. Before the manager can finish her explanation he storms out silently, pushing a man aside. His card is messaged with a short précis of the exchange. The next time he presents it the unfortunate library officer dealing with him will be warned what to expect.

Bookmark 2

A postcard of Crete inside a Jo Nesbø novel:

Dear Grandad and Grandma, I hope you are having a good time in England because we are having a very good time over here in Greece. I have been doing lots of surfing and body boarding. I managed to stand up on lots of waves. It was very hot and sunny. It was very annoying because I got stung by a wasp next to my ear. We went to a museum which was very interesting. We found a rope swing and I got rope burned. Soon we are going on an inflatable on a lake. Love Arthur.

Bee Interlude

I'm reading a book I've just discovered in the trolley awaiting re-shelving when a woman arrives at the desk to tell me, 'There's a bee dying.'

I put aside *Old English Libraries* by Ernest A. Savage with the intention that I'll return to it when I've dealt with the crisis.

The woman is a regular; one of the troubled legion: hurt eyes that, like Lucian Freud's, look like they belong to somebody else. She's always in black, head to foot. If she's not served immediately she storms to another service point, but today she seems to be mellow.

'Over there.' She points towards the Psychology section where I can see the small, black velvet mass on the carpet. The woman leads the way over, stands above it and points helpfully towards it. I take over a small piece of stiff card. The bee is tired but alive and doesn't resist when I prod it onto the card stretcher with the end of a ballpoint pen.

'I don't suppose you can put it out of the window, can you?'

'Not really.'

This is an award-winning, modern eco-building so the windows don't open. It has no air-conditioning because the temperature is supposedly self-regulating. All very well in theory, but in the summer Nonfiction is stiflingly hot.

'Don't hurt it,' the woman pleads.

'I'll do my best not to.'

The bee is huge and dormant but is twitching slightly so I can't consign it to the bin. 'I'll try and take it outside,' I tell the woman.

'Thank you.'

'Outside' is two flights of stairs away. I move towards the top of the first flight. A man approaches. 'Do you work here?' he asks me. (Despite the staff wearing identifying name tags, because of our casual clothing, customers usually ask for confirmation.)

'Yes.'

'I need help with my printing.'

'I'll be back shortly,' I promise him. 'I'm just dealing with a bee.'

'Ah.' The man peers at the bee on the card, judging whether he has more right to my time. Whatever his conclusion he retreats to wait at the service point.

The woman follows me towards the stairs. 'It's just that everybody's wearing sandals today,' she explains. 'And they'll be stung.'

'Yes.'

'But I'd hate it to be hurt.'

'I'm trying not to hurt it.'

The woman reaches the top of the stairs with me then, as if she's reached the end of a too-high diving board, she retreats backwards and leaves me to deal with the bee alone. Halfway down the first flight the flow of air over the creature begins to perk it up. By the mezzanine it's awake and is now crawling slowly towards the edge of the small piece of card. I turn the card on its edge in the hope that the steeper climb will slow the bee's progress, then, with hastened steps, I reach the ground-floor bookshop. The young man at the counter looks across at me, then down at the card.

'Bee,' I explain.

'Ah.'

As I approach the main doors it comes to life. Sniffing freedom, it looks around, lifts vertically from the card like a tiny helicopter and then flies out of the doors to freedom, dropping slightly lower until it picks up speed.

Back upstairs I'm glad to see the man with printing problems has been served by a colleague and use the mid-afternoon peace to return to my book: *Old English Libraries* by Ernest A. Savage. Ernest A. Savage is a polite and apologetic host, explaining in his introduction that he offers this book 'merely as a discursive and popular treatment of a subject which seems to me of great interest'.[5] He sounds like the sort of chap you'd happily spend a damp autumn afternoon chatting to in a small teashop in Harrogate. He mentions the unhappy circumstance of the illness of his friend (Mr James Hutt, MA), which robbed him of the chance to collaborate on the text. Lacking a co-writer, he admits that he puts the book before the public with less confidence.

Nevertheless, it's an erudite analysis of the central role monastic libraries played in the history of the institution during the Middle Ages. Chiefly housing theological and scriptural texts, to these were added later books on canon and civil law, 'So that the monastic collection may be characterized as almost entirely special and fit for Christian service, as this service was conceived by the religious.' St Bernard summed up the monastic library stock this way; they were 'the silent preachers of the divine word.' After the twelfth century, Savage writes, 'broadening influences were at work. The education given in the cathedral and monastic schools was found to be too restricted;

the monasteries, moreover, now began to refuse assistance to secular students.' This broader learning was provided in the early universities which, of course, established their own libraries.

In the fourteenth and fifteenth centuries, romances began to creep into all libraries 'save the academic', according to Savage. Monasteries allowed them in initially so that they could be copied and sold to augment the monastic income (until Gutenberg introduced movable type printing in the mid-fifteenth century, books were copied by hand). A 'romance' in medieval terms has a slightly different connotation to the one it has today. Savage lists the most common ones appearing in monastic catalogues as: 'The Story of Troy, especially Joseph of Exeter's Latin version, the great Arthurian cycle, the beautiful story of Amis and Amiloun, renowned all over Europe, Joseph of Arimathea, Charlemagne, Alexander . . . Guy of Warwick . . . and the semi-historical Richard Coeur de Lion.'

But the great majority of the population remained bookless. You couldn't just wander into a monastery or a university library and borrow one. They were too costly and rare: 'The medieval book-buyer paid more for his book on average than does the modern collector of first editions.'

But when a book won a reputation copies were produced in enormous numbers and,

> as only a few books had a comparatively large circulation, these few had a disproportionately powerful influence. The Bible was paramount. Aristotle dominated the whole mental horizon of the schoolmen. Alfred of Beverley tells us that Geoffrey of Monmouth's book 'was so universally talked of that to confess ignorance of its

stories was the mark of a clown'. So great was the influence of *Piers Plowman*, that from it were taken
watchwords at the great rising of the peasants.

I enjoy spending time in Ernest A. Savage's company and make a
note to borrow the first big potboiler – *Piers Plowman* – which
I've never read. Putting his book back on the returns trolley I
see the bee woman still at her table bent over a two-month-
old copy of the *New Statesman*. Perhaps sensing she's being
watched she looks towards me and comes over for a full report,
which I give. She then goes over to the window and stands there
for five minutes, presumably to look for evidence of her bee in
the outside world.

A Son of Anarchy

The way people approach the desk is an indicator of the tenor of the transaction that will follow. Those who arrive with three long strides from the queue tend to remain standing and aloof and hand over their books for issue or return with a brisk instruction, expecting rapid and efficient service. Overseas students (predominantly female) often arrive in pairs, both of them cramming like lion cubs together onto the single seat as they take out membership in halting English. Those with their carers usually ignore the queue altogether and, oblivious to the cries of anger from those who have been waiting, hand over their DVDs and expect them to be immediately processed. The less confident customers sidle apologetically from the queue and try to stand at the side of the desk while being served imagining they have less right to the time of the library services than everyone else.

Today, when the doors open a twenty-something man with Down's syndrome dashes to the counter. It's a warm day. The sun is out early, but he is dressed in a fully buttoned coat, a football scarf and a woollen football hat.

'Guns and helicopters!' he announces.

'Guns and helicopters?'

He points towards the DVD section.

'Ah.' It's not a great leap of deduction to work out that he wants an action DVD but his request is broad enough to encompass 80 per cent of the output of the American movie and TV industry over the past few decades. I search for 'Guns and Helicopters' on the enquiry system in the vain hope that such a title exists. No surprise that it doesn't.

'Guns and helicopters,' he says again, making a pistol of his right hand and pointing it towards me. 'Bang!'

At this point, a young female colleague arrives at the desk. 'Hello, Alan,' she says. Alan blushes and looks coyly towards the floor. 'He likes *Sons of Anarchy*,' she tells me (*Sons of Anarchy* is an American TV series based on the exploits of a Californian outlaw motorcycle club). Apparently he takes them out on a regular basis and is awaiting the release of the next season. She leads him to the boxed sets and they return with the first three series, which I issue to him. 'You're very nice,' Alan tells me and holds out his hand to shake. I take it. 'Goodbye,' he says as if we will never meet again before wandering away into the morning sun.

Just before eleven a cry goes up from the main doors.

'Call an ambulance! Any members of staff?'

Those working on the shop floor leave their posts and dash to the scene of the drama. A woman – mid-forties, thin, wearing jeans and a T-shirt, close-cropped hair – is lying inertly on the floor, her knees drawn up towards her chest. She is not moving. Her eyes are closed. Surrounding her is a semi-circle of elderly tourists wearing raincoats, cameras and backpacks. Two members of staff are already kneeling beside her. One leans down and asks if she can hear her. The woman doesn't respond. The first aider shakes her gently by the shoulder. Still no response. The first aider reaches for the woman's pulse. The woman opens her eyes and tries to find focus. Trev arrives and the onlookers fill him in.

'Need an ambulance?'

'Not at the moment,' the first aiders tell him.

Slowly, the woman comes around. She has fainted. It has happened before, she says. She is helped to her feet, and then to a seat and is attended by the first aiders until she feels well enough to leave.

The following day's postscript throws a new light onto the event when one of the young library casuals pauses by the desk to ask me if I've heard the latest on the fainting woman. I tell him I haven't. It seems that suspicions have been raised about the genuineness of the woman's condition after the CCTV of the incident was reviewed by Trev and the team. The footage revealed her walking in, looking left and right, and then, quite deliberately, lowering herself to the floor, where she adopted the recovery position before closing her eyes.

Ms Munchausen presumably got what she came in for.

Ballad of a Thin Man

Every branch library has its own atmosphere and smell and, of course, regulars. Occasional shifts in these outposts provide welcome relief from the relentlessness of the central library. Working in these satellites you soon realise that the conversation you have with some of the customers is the only human contact they will have that day – their trip to the library their only outing. They share details of the brief contacts (if any) they have had with their families and, for those with no families, details of the solitary meals they take on Christmas Day and other times of the year when those lucky enough to have loved ones spend much of the time complaining about having to spend time with them. The branch libraries allow you the time to have such conversations.

But they also have their share of eccentric and troubled customers and, given that community libraries are quieter, these customers are more visible. Late the previous night I was listening to Bob Dylan. I've only recently begun to fully appreciate Dylan and his reinventions. 'Ballad of a Thin Man', with its troubled and enigmatic progenitor, Mr Jones ('Something is happening here and you don't know what it is – Do you, Mr Jones?'), is a song I return to again and again. The song replays in my mind when one of the regular visitors to the community libraries comes in.

Today, Mr Jones (he is indeed a thin man) arrives with a gauze medical mask over his mouth. Yesterday, one of the staff sneezed, prompting Mr Jones to storm out, hand over his mouth. He has now returned with protection. When he reaches the PCs he puts his briefcase onto the table, takes out a sheet of newspaper (*Daily Mail*) and spreads it on the seat before sitting down. He takes a brief sly look towards the counter to ensure we've spotted him, but then quickly turns to the screen. As always, however, his attention is never entirely on the PC. His lizard eyes constantly dart around the room, observing and processing everything. Mr Jones is never at rest. He makes rare forays to the counter to collect his printing. On one of these forays he volunteered the information that he lip-reads and is 'an expert in body language'.

The attention he pays to the world around him has landed him in trouble in the past. He earned a ban for following female members of staff home and a number of other misdemeanours. He gives himself away deliberately to some of his victims. To one of the women who lives alone with her young daughter he remarked that she'd not put her bins out for the bin men the previous day. He lives nowhere near her. There's no suggestion that he's physically dangerous – his weapons of choice are psychological.

He visits the library three or four times a week, always using the same PC, and spends a disproportionate amount of his time online complaining about the service he's receiving in the library – usually by email to the head of libraries, head of the council or the newspapers. He takes issue with the noise levels, the imagined sleights, the psychological damage he suffers by being shouted at (this hasn't happened), children running around, the cleanliness of the toilets, the lack of a 'university education' of some of the staff members . . . and this occupies him for hours and hours.

The first time I met him was to hand over some printing. The printer is behind the staff desk and customers are obliged to come up and pay for their sheets before receiving them. I made the mistake of turning over Mr Jones' sheets to ensure there was something on them.

'Oh, no, no, no, no, no . . .' Mr Jones began. He didn't direct this towards me but towards his reflection in the window and continued in this fashion for the next couple of minutes, explaining to the window (or himself) issues of privacy, personal documents, the lack of care and sensitivity I'd demonstrated towards him and the general deficit in my people skills. I apologised. Perhaps he had a point. I assured him that were we ever to meet again I would be more careful in the way I retrieved his printing. I'd been warned about Mr Jones but had assumed the reports were exaggerated. They weren't. Paranoia also features high in his psychological profile.

His next arrival coincided with a visit from the head of the library service on one of her forays to the distant community libraries to meet the staff. After a convivial one-to-one in the staff kitchen with my colleague and then me, the manager left. As she did so. Mr Jones sprang up from his seat and demanded to know who I'd been talking to in the staffroom kitchen 'with the doors closed!' His demand was so forceful and unexpected that I told him before returning to the desk. Ten minutes later, because the library was quiet, I logged onto one of the public computers to check my emails (council employees have no access to personal email accounts on council computers). There was nothing of interest and I logged out a minute or so later and stood.

'I've emailed her,' Mr Jones announced as I passed him.

'Who?'

He named the head of the library service.

'OK,' I said.

'Because you were obviously emailing her to tell her about me.'

'Why should I do that?'

Mr Jones chose not to answer.

'I was checking my emails,' I told him.

'You should have told her I was here,' he said.

'Why?'

'Because we have regular correspondence.'

'But she came to see the staff, not the customers.'

'I've emailed her. It was clear you were discussing me.'

I returned to the desk. Shortly afterwards Mr Jones left. An hour later the phone rang and my colleague answered. It was the head of libraries reporting that the content of the private conversation in the staffroom had been reported to her by Mr Jones by email. I now understood why he'd been looking at the DVD carousel beside the staffroom door during their conversation, never having been known to take out a DVD. He'd been earwigging.

The following week he arrived angry. The library had been closed for a day for maintenance work and Mr Jones claimed he hadn't been warned about the closure and had endured a wasted journey. I explained to him that we'd posted notices both on the door of the library and at the desk for the previous two weeks announcing the closure date.

'I never come up to the desk,' Mr Jones said.

'Yes you do. You come up to the desk to collect your printing.'

'Well, I didn't see the notice.'

'I'm sorry but the notice was there – and it was also on the door.'

Mr Jones stormed back to his computer and spent the next hour angrily typing, two-fingered, and talking to himself. He left, still angry, at four o'clock as I and another staff member were putting up a number of A4 sheets around the library. These were the constituents of a quiz on ancient Greece we'd organised for a class visit the following day. We were discussing where best to put them.

It was a late opening day and we were due to close at seven. Having cashed up and turned off the computers it seemed safe to assume there would be no more customers so, at five to seven, we went to fetch our coats.

Mr Jones stormed back in, red-faced, and came immediately to the desk.

'If you're the poster expert, why were you asking her where to put the posters?' He was shaking with anger.

'The posters?'

'Earlier. When I went out you were asking her [here, he pointed towards my colleague] where to put up the posters . . . Mm? . . . Being the resident expert in the positioning of posters I'd have thought you could have done it without her help.'

I explained the nature of the school visit, the quiz, and why we'd had the discussion. Mr Jones continued to stare at me – angrily, silently – and then he left and we closed.

I said goodbye to my colleague, but she continued waiting by the door instead of going straight to the bus stop.

'I'm waiting for him to go,' she said.

'What?'

Two weeks ago he waited for her at the bus stop. It's not his bus, but he got on and followed her upstairs.

There are many such stories about Mr Jones. His earlier banning order is in a folder behind the desk. It details his misdemeanours and the fact that the order has now lapsed. Another one is being planned. Mr Jones is an unsympathetic character but perhaps deserves sympathy. He's isolated and wages wars with his neighbours and the council. The war in his head will go on until somebody helps him to win it.

Shelving McEwan

Deborah Rogers came to mind, as she often does, when I was clearing the Fiction shelving backlog. In this case it was an early novel by Ian McEwan: *The Child in Time*. Deborah was Ian's agent, and she was also mine. The memory of her could equally have been provoked by anything by Angela Carter, Kazuo Ishiguro, Peter Carey, Hanif Kureishi or many of the most significant writers of the past forty or so years. She nursed a number of them from obscurity into the public eye but she also supported many who never made it under the spotlight. What marked her out to her clients was that she didn't differentiate between her big hitters and those who brought very little into her agency's coffers. She knew the industry well and how fickle is fame, and how talent and luck and zeitgeist have to combine before any writer achieves any sustained attention.

The last time I saw her was for lunch. We met a couple of times a year to discuss the latest project. She was a great optimist. Although I'd published nine novels it had been clear for some time that the likelihood of 'breaking through' was now remote. Nobody sets out with the intention of becoming a mid-list writer but that is the destination of most. There is, so far as I know, no such thing as a bottom-list writer. For a year or so Deborah had been suggesting I write a nonfiction book. I said

I hadn't the heart to write an ironic biography of Nobby Stiles or, indeed, to sail the canals and write an ironic travel book. She said an idea would come. I would recognise it.

We said goodbye. She had lost her car keys but eventually discovered them in the folds of the restaurant seat. She could be chaotic and, like all agents, at times infuriating. Her office was knee deep in manuscript piles. She'd routinely leave her suitcase and manuscripts on trains (once due to some football fans blocking the passageway). She often suffered bizarre accidents and events, once waking up to find a young criminal at the end of her bed. She talked him out of the house. But she had a huge heart. Encountering a homeless man on the way to the theatre one night, she found him work in the post room of her agency.

She promised we would meet again soon. I thanked her for the lunch and we parted.

Two weeks later the phone rang at home in the middle of the morning. The house phone is now used almost exclusively for companies offering PPI compensation. Usually I ignore it, but that day I answered it. It was a colleague of Deborah. He'd rung, he said, because he didn't want me to hear the news from the TV or radio. He was sorry to tell me that Deborah had died, quite suddenly. Ostensibly in the best of health she'd suffered a heart attack in her car at the end of the day and had been discovered by her husband, at the wheel, parked up outside the house.

Only when I had begun to process her death did I begin to understand how much your agent knows and understands you. Deborah's intellect was impressive, but it was her emotional response to a manuscript that really marked her out. She would never insist on changes, merely ask careful questions of your characters or their circumstances: 'Do you think he would have

been her uncle?' 'Tell me more about this man's background . . .'
Questions that stuck in your mind, wormed their way into your
subconscious, where they'd be processed and turned over in that
place in your head where you write your stories – and finally
the answer would be given and the manuscript improved by it.

When I looked back on that last lunch we had together I
understood what she was telling me and I began to collect the
scraps of what I'd been jotting down of the conversations I'd
had with the people who came into the library. Perhaps there
was something in the new life I was living. Perhaps this was the
book I was supposed to be writing next.

Many people miss Deborah. But in the library she's here,
the silent, benign presence behind many of the books on the
shelves because, when the library closes each night, it's not hard
to imagine the books beginning to whisper to each other across
the aisles – millions of words uttered quietly into the darkness,
words that her authors entrusted first to her.

Periodicals

Brewer is especially twitchy today. One of the punchier rough sleepers, his mood can swing in a matter of seconds, his temper easily ignited. Today, when he comes in with the first arrivals, he pushes belligerently ahead of Wolf and the others to use the lavatory. He is, as always, wearing his black backpack, which hangs loose and low, suggesting there's little in it beyond the weight of its usual cargo of Tennent's Extra.

The library slowly fills. The factory of information begins to hum with conversation, baby cries, a police siren from the street, walkie-talkies crackling. I become aware of Brewer fifteen or so minutes later. Having performed his ablutions, he's walking towards the Periodicals section, where he habitually spends the early part of the day reading the *Daily Mail*. God forbid anyone who has got to the single copy before him. Periodicals is close to the coffee bar, which means that it tends to be less quiet than the other areas of the main floor. Brewer tolerates this – just. He has his regular seat and occasionally looks up and glowers at anybody whose voice has annoyed him. I watch him settle and open the newspaper and something else takes my attention. It's a thin, nymph-like, very aged street dweller with a Merlin-like beard and hair. He pirouettes across the library floor from the Gents, calling out: 'I haven't flushed it!', and then he is gone and peace is restored.

I take my tea break at eleven and return to the floor at eleven-fifteen to the sound of raised voices from Periodicals. This is not unusual. Outbreaks of hostility are regular and usually quickly subside. Today, it continues. Although I can't see the source of the noise I can see a number of customers looking towards the café. Something is kicking off. A female library officer dashes over to ask if I have a walkie-talkie. I do – and use it to call Facilities to come urgently to the ground floor. I make the same request on another frequency to the manager's office. The noise from the café continues. As I move towards it I see people backing away but continuing to watch the affray.

I round the corner of Periodicals and am not surprised to discover that the source of the mayhem is Brewer. His backpack is on the floor and he is squaring up to a shorter, thickset man. They are a couple of feet apart from each other and are both swearing profusely. Brewer's opponent has a thick South African accent. His heavily pregnant wife is standing behind him, trying to calm him down. He will not be calmed. Brewer taunts him. The verbal exchange continues. It seems that Brewer has taken exception to the fact that the South African visitor was talking loudly to his wife in the coffee area. Brewer impolitely suggested the couple 'Shut the f*** up.' The man, who has a fuse as short as Brewer's, decided to take Brewer on.

The man takes a stride towards Brewer. It seems unlikely, given the surroundings, that an actual fight will ensue, but Brewer lashes out and catches the man on his cheek with a right hook. This provokes a cry of shock from the man's pregnant wife and, thankfully, at that moment, Facilities arrive in the shape of not the expected Trev but Trent, a large, well-built, six-foot-four-inch Jamaican. Trent is occasionally visible wandering quietly around the library. He is ever watchful but I have always doubted what use he would be in a crisis. Confounding expectations he steps up to the mark and is enormously impressive. Somehow he manages to insert himself between Brewer and the South African man and without touching either of them, shepherds Brewer away – moving him entirely by his proximity. Both men continue to shout at each other, but the heat has diminished in the exchanges and perhaps both are a little relieved that the physical fight is over.

Brewer stops short of the exit. He reaches down to pick up his empty backpack and charges out of the library, swinging the pack around his head like a sling. This would have been intimidating had he not lost hold of the strap, causing the backpack to skid across the tiles of the bookshop floor to come to rest inertly by the display of *Tintin* picture books. Brewer retrieves his bag and hastily exits the library.

The shock waves continue to reverberate around Periodicals. The South African man is still angry and won't be placated by his pregnant wife. He announces to her and the small semi-circle of people around him that he's going outside to 'find that bastard' and 'kick his head in'.

He makes for the exit. Trent tries to calm him but he won't be calmed. Trent goes to call the police.

Thirty minutes later the South African man returns, a little calmer. His breath carries the sweet staleness of a recent cigarette. There is a small blush on his cheek where Brewer made contact with him. His wife leads him out of earshot and they talk.

The police arrive in the shape of a copper whose biceps are prominent beneath the sleeves of his capped-sleeve shirt. He canvasses witnesses, asks to see the CCTV footage and Trent leads him into the Security office.

He returns to library later in the morning to inform us that

Brewer has been arrested and is on his way to the police station. Undoubtedly he'll be back for his *Daily Mail* tomorrow or the day after.

Two days later Trev calls me over and asks me for a full account of the incident (he addresses me as 'young man' and seems to have taken a shine to me because I once wore a jumper by Fred Perry, which is, apparently, his favourite brand). He and his Facilities colleagues have been watching the altercation in slow motion on the CCTV. I tell him what I know. He tells me that the exterior CCTV footage revealed the South African man leaving the library and not, as promised, kicking Brewer's head in but actually sitting on a bench on the piazza talking to him in a civilised fashion. He offered Brewer a cigarette and Brewer accepted it. Were they in cahoots? Unlikely, but the incident provides enough gossip to last the rest of the day.

Laughter

Wednesday is the day of the week on which a Transit bus of adults with learning difficulties (currently rebranded 'Learning Disabled') arrive from their care home and take over one of the side rooms for a couple of hours. Today, they are preceded by *Sons of Anarchy* Alan on his weekly visit. He arrives at the desk, as always, with a fully buttoned coat and his woollen football hat. It promises to be the hottest day of the year so far and to mark this Alan is also wearing a hoodie beneath his coat.

He seems inordinately pleased with himself and insists on shaking my hand at the beginning of the transaction. He asks me my name, which he always does, and when I supply it he shakes my hand again. He has brought in a letter telling him that one of his reservations has come in. I take it from him. The letter dates from three months before and it's a notification that the seventh season of *Sons of Anarchy* has been put aside for him. Alan has already had season seven out three times. Because the reservation has lapsed (twenty-eight days are allowed), the DVD will not be on the shelf awaiting collection but will either be back on the rack or have already been taken out by somebody else. I tell Alan to wait at the counter and scour the shelves for the DVD. Thankfully it is there. I hold it up to show Alan. He gives me a thumbs-up and explains, 'They're my boys.'

I issue the DVD to him.

'You're very beautiful,' he tells my senior female colleague. She thanks him.

He then takes off his jacket and carefully folds it before draping it over a chair back. I wait, wondering if he's intending to strip naked. He takes off his hoodie and drapes it over the seat. He takes off his jumper and then proudly points at his black T-shirt. It's emblazoned with the *Sons of Anarchy* logo. 'My boys,' Alan repeats and then, laboriously and fastidiously, re-dresses. A lengthy queue has formed behind him. Collecting his DVD, his library card and his bag, which he slings over his shoulder, he holds out his hand to be shaken again. I shake it.

'You're very nice,' Alan says and wanders off.

Meanwhile, the Transit has arrived and the occupants are entering the library in a noisy crocodile. One peels away and takes Alan's place at the desk. Trish is in her late fifties or perhaps early sixties. She is an extremely cheery, chirpy, old-fashioned type, with thick-framed Edna Everage-style glasses and clothes (predominantly pink) that would have been fashionable in the 1950s. She returns a pile of CDs – an eclectic collection of country and western and 1970s pop. She also returns two DVDs – one is a racy gay (male) romcom with two chiselled and semi-naked men on the cover. The other is *Mamma Mia!*

'Have you seen it?' she asks me.

'*Mamma Mia!*? Yes.'

'Good, innit?'

'Very good.'

Slight pause. 'That Meryl Streep's in it.'

'Yes, I know.'

'See her on the telly?'

'When?'

'Friday?'

'No.'

'That Graham Norton. She was on that. Stayed up. We had Horlicks.'

I return the CDs and apply myself to issuing the five new ones. The first is Paloma Faith's recent offering.

'Is she married?' Trisha asks me.

'Who?'

''Er.' She points to the CD case.

I tell her that I don't know but I doubt it. The next one in the pile is Michael Jackson's *Thriller*.

'It's very sad,' she says, taking the CD and looking at the case.

'It is, yes.'

'Do you think he'll come back?' she asks.

'Michael Jackson?'

'Yes, 'im.'

'I don't think so.'

'Is your name Darren?' she asks me.

'No.'

'What is it?'

I tell her.

'Are you married?'

'Yes.'

She spots another member of staff.

'Is his name Darren?' she asks.

'Yes.'

'I don't like him,' she says.

'Why not?' I ask her.

'Is he married?' she replies.

'I don't think so.'

'He's very good looking,' Trish says and returns to the sofas with her colleagues.

Another of the party takes her place. It's a tiny, delicate, elderly woman with a thin pink raincoat and a transparent rain hat. There's no threat of rain today. She hands over her Enid Blyton book (Famous Five) and silently walks away.

I catch part of the conversation from the side room where the party has gathered around a low table of tea and biscuits. A matriarchal woman has taken a large photographic book from the shelves and is supporting it, face out, like a teacher on her knee, pointing to the colourful photos of the Yorkshire Dales. This is being done for the entertainment of the rest of the group, who respond to the comment she makes on each picture, usually a brief utterance of approval – 'Lovely', 'Beautiful', 'Nice'.

I hear one of the party, a young man, saying, 'I laughed this morning.'

A woman says: 'Really?'

'Yes, I laughed.'

'Really!'

Another member of the party leaves the table and arrives at the desk. He returns a number of Julia Roberts DVDs and has three guidebooks on California to take out.

'Julia Roberts lives in California,' he tells me.

'OK.'

'I'm going to see her.'

'Are you?'

'Yes.'

'Does she know?'

He ignores the question, instead informing me, 'I'm going to Spain and I'm going to read the guide books on the plane.'

'Good idea.'

'The California ones. She was in *Pretty Woman*.'

'Yes.'

'This is by the same director.' He holds up one of the DVDs – *The Runaway Bride*. 'Garry Marshall.'

'Really?'

'Yes. I'm going to see him too.'

'Have a good trip.'

'Thank you.'

As the group leave one of them, a small man with Down's syndrome, wearing an oversize black T-shirt, tracksuit bottoms, a pair of very large headphones, and a wide-brimmed cricket umpire's hat, accosts a young female customer as she walks in.

'Wanna be in my film?' he asks her.

She smiles and stops. 'Your film?'

The man thrusts out his right arm and affects the dynamic pose of his favourite superhero. His hat falls off. '*Superman*. At my studio.'

'I'm not sure.'

'All right.'

'But thank you,' she says.

Nordic Noir

It's Thursday and the usual crew are in. Brewer has been behaving since the last incident. He's washed his clothes and is reading his *Daily Mail* without resorting to violently attacking any of his neighbours either verbally or physically. Wolf is absent, and has been for a week or so. Joseph is making his daily visit with his daughter. She bounds ahead of him down the slope and into Children's. Startled Stewart was in on Tuesday and reported that 'the boys' had 'deigned to show their faces again' in town. He'd confronted them about the theft of his bag, but they'd denied it and he'd accepted their denial. There was, it seems, some trade-off. Stewart hinted at it but I didn't press him to explain. He looked as if he'd had little sleep the previous night.

The sewer saga continues. Facilities have discovered that the library outflow pipe is plastic (the building is relatively new) and where it meets the old Victorian sewer system there's a slight ridge between the pipes. This is where the waste is gathering and beginning to block. Plans are afoot to remedy it.

The book thief has also been spotted again but hurried out when she was clocked.

There's also an unsettling rumour going around about potential cuts to the service. Word is that the budget for the next financial year is going to be slashed by between 30 and 40 per cent. This will mean redundancies and closures.

One of the first customers at the desk is a polite, well-dressed, elderly man who arrives punctually at the same time each Thursday morning. He seems content and at peace with himself and, as he returns his single book (something light – Agatha Christie or M. C. Beaton) and takes out his new one, usually offers some titbit of information he has heard on the news. Today, the weather has caught his attention.

'It's snowing in Leeds,' he tells me, widening his eyes like Eric Morecambe, mid gag.

'Really?'

'Yes. According to the weather girl on the television.' He cranes round to look at the blazing early sun on the piazza outside. 'Snow! Can you believe it?' He shakes his head at the absurdity of the world, laughs a hollow laugh, stands, takes his book (Agatha Christie today), thanks me and leaves.

His place is taken by a tall and elegant couple in their mid- to late-thirties. Both are lean, dark-haired and blue-eyed, with very good skin and haircuts. She is wearing jeans and a cardigan, he is wearing a Sofie Gråbøl-type jumper, jeans and desert boots and a small walker's rucksack. The woman has reserved the latest Ishiguro, which is now in, and she has come to collect it. The couple are, I infer, Danish. I stand and am just about to make my way to the reserves shelf when a hollow-cheeked addict, wearing black from head to toe and sunglasses, bumps into the Danish man.

'Why did you do that again?!' the Danish man shouts at him. 'F***ing asshole!'

The addict moves off.

'I want you to call Security,' the Danish man says to me.

'Now?'

'He's done that twice before. Last time we were over there.' He points to the Fiction area (C–D).

'Ah.'

Addicts are regular users of the library. They have as much right to use the place as anybody and unless Facilities catch them in the act of jacking-up they have no power to exclude them. Facilities' office wall is adorned with their mug shots lifted from CCTV. A young man was found dead in the Gents last year, having overdosed.

Deaths in libraries are rare – one of the most famous being that of Edgar Lustgarten, a big name on film and television in the 1950s and 1960s. Now remembered for appearing in a studio resembling his own study, he narrated a number of short films depicting fictional crime stories based on true events at Scotland Yard. They began life as cinema second features although they made their way onto the small screen some years later. Myth (and Wikipedia) has it that in December 1978 Lustgarten visited the reference section of Marylebone Library and suffered a heart attack while reading the *Spectator*. He was later pronounced dead at St Mary's hospital, Paddington. There are, however, other versions of how he died. Richard Ingrams, for example, suggests his heart attack was suffered while he was walking along a street. The library death, though, seems more fitting for a man who had published his fifth crime novel, *Turn the Light Out as You Go*, earlier that year.

'He's there,' the Dane tells me. 'Be quick.'

I reach for the walkie-talkie, but the addict in black is already moving swiftly back towards the desk. There isn't time to call Facilities. Instead, I fall into step with the man in black.

'What?' he asks me.

'Are you all right?'

'Yeah. Why?' A sneer.

I shrug. The man makes for the exit. I accompany him until he leaves. I'm not sure why. I have no authority and no right to shepherd the man out, nevertheless I do.

'Asshole,' the Danish man repeats when I return to the desk.

After that the day is a routine one with a stream of largely untroublesome customers and no further dramas. An air of genial peacefulness hangs over the lower floor. No voices are raised. The only sound that regularly punctures the silence is the cappuccino milk-frother in the café – but it's unthreatening, even vaguely comforting.

I greet the next customer. Mid/late seventies, she sits down and reaches into her bag. She seems distracted. Beneath her right eye is a half-moon shaped bruise. Her right eye is bloodshot. She takes a thick paperback from her bag and puts it on the desk. It's *A Clash of Kings*, the second in the *Song of Ice and Fire* series which provided the basis of the global TV smash *Game of Thrones*.

'I'm bringing this back,' the woman says. 'But I need a new card.'

The woman's speech is slow – as if she's puzzling her way through each sentence.

'You've lost your card?'

'What?'

'You've lost your library card?'

'Oh yes. Yes, I've lost my card.'

Customers usually thaw when they borrow or return a book. However short the transaction the exchange bonds them briefly to you and you to them, but the woman is locked in her own world.

'Can I take your surname?' I ask her.

She gives it to me, along with her first name, Elizabeth. (A colleague recently took me to task for asking for a customer's Christian name. In this multi-faith country, I learned that it's no longer an accepted term – 'first name' is the form we're expected to use.)

I find the woman's account. She lives on the western edge of the city in an unloved suburb. I activate her replacement card and ask her to sign it, handing her a pen. She takes it but does not immediately sign. Instead she looks into the middle distance for a moment and only then does she turn to the card.

'Thank you,' she says.

'Just a pound then,' I prompt.

'Oh. Of course.' She reaches into her bag and takes out her purse. It's brand new. She pops the rabbit ear clasps with difficulty. They are tight and have not worn in.

'There.' She hands over her pound.

'You lost your card?' something prompts me to ask her again.

'Lost? No, I didn't lose my card.'

'No?'

'My bag was taken.'

'Stolen?' Lost cards are often the result of stolen handbags, usually having been snatched in the city centre.

'No. Not stolen. Well, not really. I mean . . .' She pauses then continues. 'I was coming out of Morrisons with my shopping and two boys pushed me over and took my bag. It was taken. My bag was taken from me.'

'I'm sorry.'

'Yes. I don't . . . Last, I mean, Tuesday. It was Tuesday. The police found them.'

'Good.'

'But they didn't have my bag.'

'I'm so sorry.' I hand the woman back her pound. 'I won't charge you for the card.'

The woman takes back the coin and stands. 'Tuesday. Yes, it was Tuesday.' Now she manages a smile. 'It's shaken me,' she says.

'I can imagine.'

'At least the weather's good,' she says. 'Sun.'

She doesn't want to tarnish my day with her experience. She's offering me hope – something to be thankful for. I don't tell her that it's snowing in Leeds.

The Mad Hatter

I catch something in my peripheral vision. It's mid-morning and the library is quiet. Sometimes on sunny days a watch-face meets the sun and a coin of light dances on the wall for a while. I return to the screen of my PC having noticed Wolf leaving the Gents. He has a new jumper – blue – but he is again dishevelled and filthy. He is talking quite animatedly to himself but the conversation is a happy one. Brewer is reading the *Mail* alone, slightly hunched over one of the low tables.

An unfamiliar street sleeper in an Army jacket has joined the throng but he doesn't know the rules. He's so drunk he can barely hold up his head. He arrives at the desk and asks for his library number because he's lost his card and he wants to use the computer. His account is locked because he owes over £50 in fines due to unreturned books. I explain this to him and he asks if that means he can't use the computer. I tell him that I'm afraid he can't. If, however, he wants to pay off the fine, or at least set up some kind of payment plan, then I can unblock the card. He chooses not to respond but returns to the chair beside the PC. His huge bag is behind it. Facilities have already clocked him and when he sits down I see two of them approach him. One of them kneels down and they talk to him quietly. He doesn't seem to hear them but he leaves.

Again something catches my eye. I look up to see a tiny, wiry man, almost frantically running from shelf to shelf and chatting rapidly to himself. He's on a Mad Hatter's mission. Was he not a customer his industry could have been that of one of the staff, busily looking for reserved books or tidying the shelving – although perhaps he is moving far too fast for a staff member. This elderly man is doing the opposite. When he reaches a shelf he looks from right to left, then top to bottom, and then, seemingly at random, pulls a book from one of the shelves. He has a stash of them on one of the seats and he places the new book on the top of the pile, which he then picks up with difficulty (he has a large leather bag in his other hand) and transports to another chair, losing two or three books from the top of the pile in the process. I watch him, fascinated. His face is gaunt with deep-grained lines. He is stooped almost double and must be approaching his mid-eighties. He is wearing a large, dark blue suit jacket which must in earlier years have fitted him, beneath it a loose grey cardigan and tracksuit bottoms. Facially he brings to mind Samuel Beckett in those haunting black and white photos in which he stares imperiously towards the camera, his craggy face lined deep.

Now the Mad Hatter is hidden from my sight behind the Fiction shelving (J). I leave my PC to see what he's up to. His stash of eight or nine books is piled on the triangular seat beside him; three of them are on the floor. He is peering into his blue, fake leather shopping bag and talking animatedly. From it he takes out a length of toilet roll and wraps one end around his wrist, the other around the handle of his bag. He then begins to secrete the books in his bag. On this evidence the man is a book thief but something stops me from radioing Facilities to report him; something about his behaviour is too erratic.

He stands, leaving a messy mass of litter around his chair, and heads for the doors. But then something seems to stop him and he turns left and lifts his heavy bag onto the counter beside one of the library staff. Wordlessly he begins to take the books from his bag and pile them on the counter beside her. Rather than a random selection I see that he's chosen a selection of sturdy literary gems by Saul Bellow, Virginia Woolf, Isaac Bashevis Singer and Henry James. His bag now devoid of the books, my colleague asks him if he'd like them issued. She looks at him with some concern and sympathy. He nods, but he can't find his card in the chaos of his bag. He returns to his seat and my colleague embarks on serving another customer. The man is becoming more fractious, frantically rummaging through his bag. I approach him. Without looking up he says, 'Thank you.'

'For . . .?'

'Sending back my bus pass last week.'

'OK.'

The Mad Hatter takes out a pink leather bus pass wallet and holds it up. Somebody else on the staff must have found it and posted it to him. Intending to return it to his bag, instead he drops it on the floor, along with some other residue. I kneel to collect it. The litter comprises a number of torn and stained till receipts, a raffle ticket from the previous summer for a horse charity, a postal order for £1.46, a letter informing him he has won £15,500 in a prize draw and has only to call a number to collect it, and several expired bus tickets.

'I'm exhausted,' he tells me. 'Exhausted.' For a moment he pauses. Then he goes on: 'She's at home watching *Last of the Summer Wine* . . . Well, you can understand why.'

'Are you looking for your library card?' I ask him.

'Yes. Yes.'

'Shall I help?'

'Yes. I'm exhausted.'

I offer sympathy.

'I saw four drunks today. Four! They asked me for money. I go to Spain with a friend and my wife. Spain and Portugal.' His voice is cultured. He goes on, making random connections between incidents in his life in Spain and drunks he has encountered on the streets.

He removes another length of toilet roll from his bag and then sits back, trying to get his breath back, inviting me to look inside. I lift it onto the seat and open it. His bag contains an ancient, sealed packet of coconut creams, a large, empty plastic bag, several torn envelopes and a pristine china teacup and saucer, but no library ticket.

While I'm looking for his card he stands and returns to the issues desk to collect his books. My colleague asks him for his ticket. He looks towards me and tells her he can't find it. Frustration surfaces and he begins to hit the right side of his brow hard with his clenched fist. The woman reaches out and gently takes his hand, guiding it back down to the counter. As she holds his hand, his fist slowly relaxes. He looks at her as if he has seen her for the first time. She explains that she can issue the books if he gives her his name and address. Her gentleness calms him. I take his bag to the desk and we put the books in.

'I'll have to find a cab,' he says. 'I can't manage the bus.'

I ask him if he'd like me to call one for him. He tells me he would. I take him back to his seat and call a local company, who tell me the cab will be there shortly. I return to the man and offer to help him to the doors. He thanks me and reaches up for my arm. He takes it and I can feel the strength of his grip through my sleeve.

'How tall are you?' he asks me.

I tell him I'm around five-foot-eleven but feel as though I have shrunk recently. We walk out of the library arm in arm and the cab arrives a moment later. I open the back door but the Mad Hatter says he doesn't want to travel in the back, but will sit up front beside the driver. Cheerfully, the driver agrees to his request. As we walk around the back of the cab we are narrowly missed by a muscular, one-legged man in a wheelchair moving at speed down the centre of the narrow street. On his right knee is the red scar of the operation which presumably recently removed the lower part of his leg. He is wearing a black capped-sleeve T-shirt and black running shorts. His head is shaved. He calls an apology. The cab drives off.

I found Matthew Battles' *Library: An Unquiet History* a couple of days ago on one of the returns trolleys and took it out. The Mad Hatter's teetering pile of literature leads me to a brief diversion into this illuminating book, which prompted memories of junior school lessons about papyrus and vellum and how the Romans employed armies of copyists to write their speeches, decrees, commercial documents and histories. Battles reminds us that after the fall of the Roman Empire little was being written for permanent record. It was the religious communities who continued the practice, inscribing the scriptures onto wax tablets:

It was probably from such wax tablets that Coptic monks in Egypt had first taken the inspiration to invent, or at least to perfect, the form of the book as we know it today: the codex . . . it has been speculated that the English word 'book' in fact comes from the Anglo-Saxon word for beech (*boc*), the favoured material from which the panels of tablets were fashioned. The panels typically were carved with a shallow reservoir into which beeswax could be poured; cool, the beeswax made a soft surface into which letters could be inscribed with a sharp stylus . . . Often two such panels were joined together with cord.[6]

Three hours after the departure of the Mad Hatter and his stash of literature I am summoned to the phone at the main desk. The caller is a woman who asks if I helped a 'confused, elderly man' find a cab. Sensing a problem, I tell her that I did. She asks if he had a £20 note on him. I tell her that I didn't see one, but it would have been likely that he might, at some point, have lost it, given the chaos of the circumstances. She thanks me and then tells me that she's become increasingly concerned about him; that it's likely that he will have to return to hospital. I offer my sympathies and give her the number of the cab company I called. She thanks me again and hangs up.

Curriculam Vitay

A late-middle-aged, formally dressed woman in an inexpensive business suit dashes up to the Nonfiction enquiries desk to announce that her PC booking is about to run out and she needs more time. A free hour per day is allowed. Her hurried explanation is that she's typing up her brother's CV and has not quite finished. He needs a job and has asked her to help him because his spelling is poor. I extend the booking by fifteen minutes and the woman dashes back to her PC, which is in the IT Suite, off the main room. Peace is restored and I spend five minutes helping a student look for books with botanical illustrations.

Bizarrely, and coincidentally, a young Spanish man then visits the desk to ask me to look at his CV (this is not uncommon). It's impressive and paints a picture of a decently qualified economist who has worked in a number of financial institutions in Spain – albeit as an intern. I make a few suggestions and the man then asks me to look at his covering letter, which I say I'm happy to do. He finds it on his iPhone and I read it. I suggest some reordering. The young man thanks me profusely and leaves the desk.

Ten minutes later the woman dashes back to the service point, this time trailed by her brother – similar age, very well shaven, dark, smart jacket, smart slacks, military haircut and very dry lips. His smart clothing, like hers, belongs to the 1980s. There's perhaps formality in the parentage – lower middle management – gentility, maybe, a few generations back. A rum, Patrick Hamiltonesque anti-hero. He's on his mobile phone, making sure he's just out of earshot. The woman asks for help to print out her document. I follow her and her brother back to her PC. The document, two pages long, is entitled Curriculam Vitay. I confirm that the document is ready for printing. The woman concurs but says, 'I haven't had time to do a spellcheck.'

A difficult moment – a moral question. Choose one of the three below, do you: Suggest she does a spellcheck? Offer to do one for her? Tell her to print anyway?

It's a minute before twelve – my lunch break, and I'm sorely tempted to go for option three. Instead I opt for option two. This is not entirely altruistic. I have become interested in the man skulking in the background and am intrigued to learn more about his work record. The CV has four or five literals in it, but not as many as I snobbishly suspected it would have. The man has six GCSEs and has done a number of short-term jobs – mainly postal delivery jobs, which he has listed as 'Postal deliveries'. Under his section 'Skills', he has put 'delivering post'.

'Perhaps you could fill this out a bit,' I suggest. His sister agrees, turning to him and saying, 'I told you we should do that.' He holds up his hand, palm out, not wanting to be interrupted mid phone call.

We work on building his profile. By the end of it he has an impressive skill list: excellent customer-focused service skills, route planning, prioritising workload, interpersonal skills, cash handling, etc.

I'm intrigued by an entry that suggests he worked in an east London florist's fifteen years before. The job is listed as 'Florist', duties, 'flowers'.

'What did you do?' I ask the man.

Instead his sister answers. 'He did the wreaths and stuff. Didn't you?'

The man nods.

'No training. He used to do all the floral tributes . . . for the boys.' She looks at the man fondly. He enjoys the flattery. I sense it's rare.

There's a long gap in his CV – around nine years. I'm tempted to ask the reason but I don't because I think I already know the answer.

I tell the man I'm impressed by his six GCSEs and two A levels. There's a moment's pause before his sister snorts derisively and offers a coy look towards her brother. 'Oh, he hasn't got any qualifications.'

'None?'

'No, love, but you have to put something down, don't you?'

I choose not to offer a response. The document is printed, two copies, and, for the first time the man speaks, announcing to his sister that he is going to the pub to meet a man called Graham. She can join them if she likes.

A Blockage

The sole topic of conversation on Monday morning as the library is being set up (accompanied by the soundtrack to Isaac Hayes' *Shaft* soundtrack) is the manhole incident. According to Trev, late on Saturday afternoon, the manhole lifted outside Pizza Express and began to pour human waste into the piazza. The sewers had backed up, putting all of the toilets in the library out of operation. Facilities stayed late to clear the blockage, literally shovelling s**t into a bucket and depositing it down a drain. It wasn't, Trev admitted, the best Saturday night he'd ever had. Facilities were praised by management and the manhole incident went into the annals of library folklore.

A week and a half later it happens again. This time I am on duty so I live through the drama first hand. The first sign of it is water pouring out of a drain in Children's. Facilities are called and another sewer blockage is diagnosed. Toilets (public and staff) are flushed but the waste remains resolutely in the toilet bowl. The unfolding drama is monitored on the Facilities channel on the walkie-talkies. Throughout the library, reports of flushing – and the results of the flushing – are broadcast.

'Downstairs disabled. Flushing now.' A pause, and then: 'Nothing's coming through.'

'Upstairs staff. Flushing now.' Ditto.

'A' boards are hastily erected. The public are bing-bonged on the tannoy and the announcement is made that no toilet facilities are available in the building. Staff who had been holding on to the next tea break become ashen faced. A manager circulates the service points and explains that should any staff member need to go to the toilet, their service point will be covered and Starbucks have agreed we can use their facilities.

The drama continues to unfold. At four o'clock two men arrive wearing dark blue T-shirts and thick rubber gloves – the blockage experts. Grim-faced, they skirt the barriers and enter the ground-floor Gents, only to emerge looking even more grim-faced.

'We're sending a camera down,' we hear on the walkie-talkie. Excitement is growing – among the staff it's like listening to Orson Welles' *War of the Worlds* drama on radio.

The camera goes down and the blockage is reported coyly by the female head of Facilities. She suggests that it could be imagined what was contained in it but that the emergency drain men would try to flush it out. The fear is that there will be a backlash, unleashing a literal tidal wave of human waste into the library. A promising scenario for a new disaster movie is unfolding.

We wait.

The flushing begins. It is soon reported that the blockage has been cleared. The staff are grateful that they can again use the toilets, but feel slightly flat that the drama is now over.

That's Why I'm Here

'Do you work here?'

'Yes, I do.'

'Do you mind if I ask you a question?' It's an elderly man –
late seventies, myopic, sky-blue watercolour irises, filthy-lensed
glasses. He is short – around five feet – and is wearing a white
sailor's cap and a rubber jacket that smells of fish.

'You see I have trouble with my memory,' he says. 'I can
remember things from the past, for example shops, but I can't
remember what I did yesterday.'

I nod encouragingly.

'Sometimes I have to ask people what day it is.' He smiles:
'Wednesday.'

'Wednesday?'

'The last time I asked it was Wednesday.'

'It's Monday today,' I tell him.

'Is it?'

'Yes.'

As he registers the day his eyes squint briefly, then he goes on:
'So what I'd like to ask is why the automatic returns machines
don't tell me if I've had a book out before?'

'Ah. I see.'

'Yes, you see if I go to the counter, then they can tell me, but if I go to the machine, it doesn't. It's very frustrating.'

I concede the point and tell him I'll raise the issue with the IT team.

'And then when I get home and start the book I realise I've read it.'

'Yes, I see the problem.'

This is not uncommon – the more elderly borrowers regularly discover they have borrowed books before. On learning, some of them cluck or tut and apologise and make some comment about failing memory, while others press on anyway, arguing that if they can't remember the title they might not remember the plot. Others enjoy re-reading books like children – it's comforting, no nasty narrative surprises; like meeting an old friend and going through past times together.

'I read a lot of le Carré,' the myopic man says. 'But you see I can't remember what I've read. So if your machine told me then I'd know.'

I concede the point again. 'Thank you,' I tell him and begin to move away, assuring him for the second time that I will raise the issue with IT. He follows me.

'You see, if the machine told me . . .' He runs through his concern again, word for word. I listen to it for the third time. He comes to a close and it looks as if he's finished. I thank him again.

'I hope you don't mind me telling you.'

'No, I don't mind.'

There must have been some frustration on my face because I see a wince of regret, perhaps embarrassment, register in the old man's eyes.

'Well, thank you,' he says and walks away towards the automatic issues/returns machines. I feel a pang of guilt, but I don't have time to listen to the man's story for a fourth time. Or perhaps I do. Perhaps that's why I'm here.

I'm pondering this as I return to the service point, and it's there I glimpse the Mad Hatter. He's taking out a book at the counter. His hair has been cut brutally short and he looks like a different man. The air of chaos is gone. He's more upright. The conversation he is holding is rational and focused. He has a new jacket on and grey canvas deck shoes – Vans – ridiculously contemporary. Can it be the same man? It is. I wander over and say hello.

He looks at me without recognition, without a smile or reply, and then he leaves.

The Dice Man

An urbane man. An academic type. Luxuriant grey hair, centre-parted in 1970s soft-rock fashion, a black Nehru jacket, good jeans, tortoiseshell thick-rimmed glasses and the two-glasses-of-red-wine-on-an-empty-stomach drawl of the media industry. He is, or has been, in charge of people and he's used to his opinions being taken seriously. He sits down, places a small paperback on the desk, squares it up with his fingertips, and, in the way of a university lecturer, begins: 'Let me ask a question.'

'Of course.'

'Who chooses the books?'

This is a tricky one. The answer is loaded because the truth is that a central wholesaler supplies the books. Until recently around 50 per cent of these were selected in-house by the stock team, and the remaining 50 per cent by the wholesaler. The books arrive almost daily in cardboard boxes, packed carefully in brown paper padding, already labelled, slip-cased, barcoded and logged on to the computer system (i.e. 'shelf ready'). One of the ongoing tasks for the staff allocated an hour in the 'Workroom' is to 'discharge', i.e. return the books to enter them onto the system, and, in so doing, ensure the title the system has for each of them is correct. There were two stock-buyers on the staff. These were experts in their field. Their job was to keep an

eye on the slow-moving books, to 'weed' out the non-movers
and dog-eared, to ensure there was shelf space for the new stock
and, primarily, to supply appropriate books to the library's users.
One had responsibility for fiction, the other for nonfiction. The
stock of a library is an organically developing entity. The books
'weeded' are, first, deleted from the system, then the title page
taken out and the book either put out to be sold or sent to one
of the charitable book-reclaiming services.

I précis this process to the urbane man.

'I only ask,' he says, not remotely interested in the answer I
have offered, 'because this book was so execrable I'm surprised
it's on the shelf. It seems to have been written by some gauche
twenty-year-old. Positively bloody awful.'

I take the book from him. 'Ah,' I begin.

He raises his eyebrows.

'Self-published,' I announce.

The exceptions to the incoming stock strategy are the
self-published books. Once called 'vanity publishing', since the
democratisation of the industry anybody can now get their
memoirs published and an ISBN number to go with it for a relatively reasonable sum. Many of these are gifted to the library
and because the library has a policy of supporting local authors,
a number of these end up on the shelves. This is one of those
books. I explain this to the man. He's content – relatively – but
he's got something to get off his chest and he's going to do it: 'I
did this thing, you see. I decided to walk round blindly – well,
with my eyes open – and then stop, pick up a book and take it
home and read it. Like *The Dice Man*, Luke Rhinehart – you've
probably not read it.' (I have.) 'Luck of the draw. This is the book
I took.' He stands. 'Well, I won't be doing it again.' His concluding expression suggests that I'm not only solely responsible for

the library's stock-buying process, but also for the contents of the execrable book written by the gauche twenty-year-old.

'Thanks for the warning,' I say as the urbane man leaves.

But his question has been concerning me for some time. Given the fact that the incoming stock is provided by a massive conglomerate I'm prompted to look up the company. Their website boasts that they are 'a leading specialist supplier of shelf-ready books and multimedia to public libraries and schools in the UK and around the world'. They began as a small book-supply business operating out of an old chicken shed. Now, they 'proudly operate in over 100 countries' and their buying power – and the power they hold over the publishing industry and the reading public – is, therefore, awesome. As the debate over the pros and cons of libraries goes on, one of the major cons (regularly trotted out by the government) is that the internet now supplies the information we once found in library books. Contrary to this position, the writer Caitlin Moran, launching her 'Save the libraries manifesto', recently had this to say: 'Why do we need libraries, I hear you cry, when there is the internet? Well, the thing about the internet is that it'll only show you what's most popular, not what is best.'

So one of the major lines of defence is that libraries supply 'what is best'. But do they? The 'improving' imperative of the fledgling public libraries was a big issue in the 1870s. The American reformer Melvil Dewey (who we'll meet again later) is remembered for his eponymous metric nonfiction classification system. What is less well known are his contributions to what public libraries in the USA should have on their shelves and how it should be curated. He was instrumental in defining the new profession of public 'librarian' and, as if that wasn't time-consuming enough, belonged to a group of spelling reformers who were in favour of modifying words, such as dropping the silent 'e', using 'u' in any words with a long 'u' sound, 'through' for example, and substituting 'f' for 'ph'. Their argument was that this would make English easier to learn and reduce the time children needed to spend at school.

The platform for Dewey and his gang was a new publication, the *American Library Journal*, the first issue promoting a conference on libraries as well as an article by him on 'The Profession', which summarised his views of what a librarian should be. Here's Wayne A. Wiegand on Dewey:

> He noted the best librarians were 'positive aggressive characters' who stood 'in the front rank of the educators of their community, side by side with the preachers and the teachers.' Because people increasingly obtained their ideas and motivation from reading, and because 'this influence may be wielded most surely and strongly through our libraries,' librarians had a responsibility to make it easy for readers to elevate their reading tastes, and in the process teach them about prudent self-selection. 'Children of the lower classes' who had to leave school for work at an early age often subsequently developed 'bad reading habits' – a taste for dime novels and story papers. The library had to counter this by supplying reading 'which shall serve to educate'.[7]

As public libraries proliferated on both sides of the Atlantic, panels of the great and the good were established to choose what would go on the shelves. But how is the stock dictated today?

Until recently the two in-house stock experts had autonomy over what they buy to supplement the stock delivered by the wholesaler. The wholesaler sent the fiction-stock expert a 'virtual basket' each month from which she selected the books she wanted. The other way stock can find its way onto the shelves is if a borrower requests that we buy it. If the book is considered to have a reasonably broad appeal then the request is usually complied with, the book ordered and delivered to the library.

The two stock experts lost their jobs in the recent changes and their responsibilities incorporated within the responsibilities of two other managers. The nonfiction specialist was asked to write a 'stock profile' for the wholesaler. It will be used by them as they take more responsibility in selecting the stock. As for fiction, in the past the wholesaler supplied only mass-market fiction. It's expected that in the future they will supply a large percentage of the fiction stock. There's no question that their influence over what will be available on the shelves will increase. As it does, the argument over libraries supplying 'what is best' over 'what is popular' loses traction.

There's no indication on the wholesaler's website to suggest how they choose the books they supply to libraries – so I called their main switchboard and asked to talk to one of their stock-buying team. I was given an email address which I used. In return I was told that my communication would be forwarded to somebody higher up in the chain. Two weeks later, after no reply, I emailed again to be told that I would be contacted. I wasn't. A further email was not responded to, so the supply policy remains mysterious.

Let's Be Careful Out There

Monday's staff briefing plays out like the opening scene in the seminal NBC cop drama *Hill Street Blues*. Aficionados will remember that after the roll call and the day's advisories ('Let's spend a little less time flirting with hookers and waitresses and put some heavy attention on that park'), Sergeant Esterhaus routinely closed with what would become a TV catchphrase: 'Let's be careful out there.' *Hill Street Blues* was significant in that it schooled a number of American film and TV writers who went on to develop some of the most enduring series on the networks.

This morning, the library's own Esterhaus runs through the events of Saturday. It was a busy one for staff and Security. First off, somebody on the ground floor stole another badonger, the tag remover for DVDs, and the keys to the automatic issues/returns machines. Someone spotted him making off with the keys and the alert went out to look for a tall, well-dressed gentleman with silver hair. The suspicion is that he's a professional thief, not one of the usual sneak-thief chancers. Facilities don't know him so his mug shot is not yet up on their wall. CCTV is checked and this is remedied with a duplicate copy pinned on the staffroom noticeboard.

Meantime, the bookstore thief is back and Esterhaus announces, after a dramatic pause, that she has been apprehended (applause from the gathered staff). Although she had been spotted on CCTV helping herself to the stock in the shop three or four times, she has never been caught at it. On Saturday, the eagle-eyed member of staff on the bookstore till saw her skulking around the shelves. Facilities were radioed and her collar was felt. The police were called and she was taken to the office to wait for their arrival. Over an hour later they turned up and questioned her. The outcome was that the thief, who has mental health issues for which she is receiving treatment, has agreed to repay the cost of the goods and she has written a letter of apology. She is very sorry.

A known mobile-phone thief is back. Her modus operandi is to approach somebody working at one of the tables (usually an overseas student), looking distressed and holding a sheet of A4 paper. While engaging the customer in conversation she covers the mobile phone with the sheet of paper. When she moves off, the phone is removed from the table camouflaged by the paper. Today, she's back with a male accomplice and is being watched carefully.

While she is being monitored, the badonger thief is back and is immediately spotted. Facilities are radioed. The thief somehow realises he has been clocked and heads for the exit, rapidly (ish) trailed by the duty manager and another member of staff. They catch him up halfway down the street. Coolly he listens to the accusation. He doesn't care. He's a professional. The duty manager suggests that if he returns to the library he will be 'toast'. Esterhaus would have been proud.

Joseph arrives in long canvas shorts, waddling as he follows his daughter into Children's. He looks like he is wearing a full nappy. His smile is in place – but occasionally it slips. He is soon talking to two women from the distance of a seat – they are on the floor mats. Consciously or not he is giving them permission not to include him. His daughter is running along one of the long cushions and for the first time I see that because he is excluded from the herd, so is she. When he runs after his daughter, or she runs after him, he is her only playmate. She doesn't engage with the other children, indeed seems barely to be aware of them. The women are exchanging advice on sore lips – advice handed down to them. They are sharing more than information – the tone is low and intimate. Occasionally, in one of the pauses, a woman offers some incident of vulnerability to the group. They listen and they respond. One is talking about her husband. They have all had the experience she mentions – unfeeling, unseeing. She seems relieved. Joseph looks on. Sometimes he manages to join the circle and offer some moment in his daughter's life. The women listen politely, for a few moments including him, and then they turn away and Joseph returns his attention to his child.

When the Moribund
Fall to the Street

As the summer continues Facilities have the daily job of putting out the deckchairs on the AstroTurf lawn adorning the piazza outside the library. They also wheel out two ping-pong tables which are stored in the library entrance. The area is hugely popular at lunchtimes with the local workers and the language students who routinely block the narrow pavements of the city throughout the summer months. The piazza is also popular with the seagulls.

Herring gulls have changed. Nowadays they are more brazen – staring you out should you have the temerity to be eating a sandwich on an outdoor bench. They no longer respond to shooing: they just retreat a few steps and continue staring thuggishly, waiting for a moment's inattention. A local café has taken to putting up blackboards outside its premises explaining that they are not responsible for the seagulls' behaviour. Another café provides plastic covers for the plates, which it encourages customers to use between mouthfuls. June is a particularly trying month – this is the time that the young are born and while the mothers tend them on flat roofs and chimney stacks, the fathers circle the city, dive bombing for food. In between times they perch on chimney pots, necks extended, beaks wide open, shouting insanely at the clouds.

This year the papers are reporting the growing threat. A Yorkshire Terrier and a tortoise have, apparently, both been killed by gulls and OAPs are regularly reported to be startled by them. This city considered a cull a couple of years ago. The yellowing council notice announcing it is still there on one of the library staff noticeboards. For a couple of Sundays, they were to offer a bounty for each dead seagull delivered to them. It was not a spoof notice – it was a genuine project. The cull, however, was ruled out following a last-minute report that admitted the gulls 'are capable of making a round trip of 100 km in search of food in only a few hours' and 'are considered more intelligent than most'. The writer also offered the astute observation that: 'The discharging of firearms in built-up areas will have safety implications. The poisoning of birds will engage the minds of the health and safety executive, not only for operatives, but also for passers-by when the moribund fall into the street.'

Finally, the council also acknowledged that 'Britain is a nation of animal lovers' and ultimately this put them off culling seagulls. No mention was made that herring gulls are on the red endangered list and so the bizarre notion of dozens of bounty hunters with shotguns wandering through the city on a Sunday morning taking potshots at the birds was also illegal.

Today, a child in a pushchair is wheeled into Children's with a clearly distressed mother. The mother arrives at the desk and empties the contents of a voluminous shopping bag. 'I'm bringing these back,' she announces and then returns her concern to her daughter, who is sitting silent and glassy-eyed in her pushchair.

I return the books and ask the mother if there's anything else I can do. She thanks me and says there's nothing else, but she seems reluctant to leave. I ask her if she's OK.

'We were coming down the street,' she says. 'My daughter was eating a sandwich in her pushchair and a seagull swooped down and took it out of her hand . . . she didn't cry.' Again she looks at her daughter. 'But she hasn't said anything since.'

The woman wheels the pushchair up the exit slope to face the potential terror on the streets.

Trending Orange

The morning's staff briefing is almost inaudible due to a police helicopter circling low overhead. Two buses have collided in the city centre and there are casualties. When the helicopter moves off we're told that the crime spree in the library continues and the mobile thief is now working with a gang. We should be vigilant. The second item is that silver wraps have been found in the Gents, suggesting the cubicle is again being used by one of the customers shooting up. It's also announced that one of Britain's fading comedians is going to mount an hilarious stunt soon after we open and we should be aware. There is then some discussion as to whether we, as staff, should have been tipped the wink given that this appears to be a *Candid Camera*-style set-up in which hapless members of the public will be made to look stupid for the amusement of the viewers.

At around half past ten a man with a head-mounted camera on his cycle helmet rides in. He is wearing a light green scarf around his mouth and sunglasses. He cycles around the library for a while, ignored by most people, and then finally a member of staff who has arrived after the briefing stops him and tells him to dismount. The hilarious incident is caught on camera. A release form is proffered by the producer, and the comedian then leaves to continue the hilarity elsewhere in the city.

This being Wednesday, the care-home outing has arrived and taken up residence in the side room. The low tables are laden with the usual array of biscuits and tea flasks. One of the party, a young woman in a wheelchair, is crying loudly and one of the carers is kneeling beside her, offering reassurance. The others are unperturbed. Unlike in the other world, happiness and sadness, openly expressed, are considered natural behaviour. Trish is up and is cheerily bustling around her colleagues. She spots me and waves. I wave back and go over to say hello.

'I know you,' Trish says. 'Don' I?'

'Yes.'

'What's your name?'

I remind her.

'You married?'

'Yes.'

'You look very nice,' she says, looking approvingly at the beach shorts and black T-shirt (dress code is informal).

'Thank you.'

'Is your name Darren?'

'No.'

It's a quiet day. The humidity of the past week has declined and the temperature is more bearable with a welcome breeze coming in low through the main doors and cooling feet and legs. An elderly woman approaches the desk in a thick coat and scarf.

'Have you moved the Ds?' she asks.

I tell her that we haven't. They're still rooted between C and E. She looks confused so I lead her over to the shelf and she finds her book by Barbara Delinsky.

A man with a dirt-grained face comes and leans on the desk. He reeks of fresh alcohol and stale sweat.

'Just got sent home. Cooling fan's gone down.' No further explanation is offered.

'Excellent,' I say.

'Can you give me my library number? I know my pin. Need to use the internet.'

He gives me his surname and shows his bank card.

'Will you get paid?' I ask him.

'Yeah. Result.'

'Result indeed.'

'Got to take it as leave, though.'

'Oh.'

'Still. Afternoon off.'

'Absolutely.'

'Cheers then.'

'Cheers.'

In the later morning, Startled Stewart makes a brief appearance. He has a new leather man bag across his arm. His fake tan has darkened to the sheen of a conker, his hair is even blacker than the impossibly black it was the last time I saw him, and he is wearing an incredibly bright, predominantly orange kaftan – rather like those favoured by post-release Mandela. He looks across at me and smiles, and zips over.

'Oh, hello,' he says – and then spots a very good-looking Italian student on the way to the Gents.

'I'm just in for a wee,' he says and shoots off in hot pursuit.

I spend the latter part of the afternoon upstairs in Nonfiction. The area is bright and quiet. The phone rings. I answer it. A well-spoken elderly man begins a long preamble about the internet and I sense that this will be a long call.

'You see, I don't use the internet,' he says, 'I hope you don't mind helping me . . . you're usually very helpful.'

I tell him I'll do what I can.

'I live in sheltered accommodation. I've had a couple of breakdowns but I'm all right now.'

'That's good.'

'You sound like an educated man.'

'Well . . .'

'And people there are always very accommodating when I phone up.'

Pause.

'I'm interested in politics, you see. I write to the papers. I embarked on joining Twitter but I decided not to go through with it. There might, however, be some residual account with my name on it.'

Pause. I prod him on. 'OK . . . what can I do for you?'

'I think . . . I mean, the issue is that some of the opinions I hold I know aren't popular with certain parties: the government, for example. ISIS. I don't want to end up like Lee Rigby.'

'Of course not. Who would?'

'So the reason I'm calling . . .'

At last.

'I wonder if you could do a quick internet search to see if my name is mentioned.'

'You're concerned that . . .?'

'I'm being discussed.'

'Ah. On the internet?'

'Yes. On social media.'

He gives me his name and his address. I search and find relatively few people with the same name – a couple of LinkedIn accounts, but nothing interesting, remarkable or relevant. I share the results of my search.

'Could you look on Twitter?' he asks.

I look, but not having a Twitter account I tell him my access is limited. I type in his name but can find nobody listed.

'So you can't tell me what's trending?'

'Do you think you might be trending?'

'Possibly.'

'I see.'

I assure him that this is unlikely. The conversation continues, shifting into more general paranoid concerns.

He ends with the assurance that he'll call the BBC. Apparently they're always very obliging when he calls to ask them to check out Twitter. I wish him well.

The peace on the piazza is then shattered by the dull rhythmic bump of bass. I wander over to the tall windows and see that a drinks company has invaded the AstroTurf. Part of it is cordoned off by ropes. Within the cordon are a number of tables and a garish gazebo and free drinks are being dished out by attractive young people in orange T-shirts from a large orange caravan. The regular users of the AstroTurf have been confined to a strip of about twenty feet by the road.

The deafening thump of the music tortures the silence for the rest of the afternoon and presumably goes on into the night.

Never Pet a Burning Dog

The library, being the modern equivalent of the village pump, is now pretty much the only place in the city that anyone can wander into and find something to do or somebody to talk to. Being so, it's a barometer of the mood of the city and sometimes when you arrive you sense the mood is an unsettling one. Today is one of those days. Primal Scream is playing from the CD as the library is set up. The staff are generally silent, waiting for the caffeine to kick in. The mood is sombre.

At the morning briefing the latest news on the sewer is that a recent camera sortie discovered an unused conduit under the piazza which is now a holiday home for the local rat population. Discussions are ongoing.

I'm soon on my way to Children's, where a ginger-haired child is having a major temper tantrum. He has been told by his mother not to put his hand into the mouth of the returns bin and he has taken exception to the admonishment. He is now lying on his back, lifting and dropping his feet onto the floor and screaming loudly. The woman arrived with a friend and her son, who approaches the ginger-haired child and stands on his chest. Mother two dashes over and addresses the child:

'That's very naughty, Roscoe. It's very naughty to stand on people!'

Roscoe, unperturbed, wanders off. The ginger-haired child's anger burns out and peace returns. Meanwhile, the other library officer on duty in Children's wanders over to inform me that a child has 'exploded'. Closer inspection reveals she has projectile vomited her breakfast against one of the pillars. Facilities are alerted.

At the next shift change I'm on the main desk. The first customer is a Chinese woman who arrives and asks about a photographic exhibition. I tell her that the exhibition has finished. She asks me when it finished. I make up a date – it's irrelevant, surely? She presses me on the date. I concede that the date is approximate, I don't know when the exhibition finished (and care even less). The fact remains that it is no longer there. The Chinese woman (still standing) then slowly begins to unpack the entire contents of her large bag onto the desk. She does this silently, without explanation, as a queue builds behind her. When she has finished she asks me about the service the library provides to help people with computer literacy. I explain how she can sign up with a volunteer and ask her if she's a library member.

'Yes,' she says, 'have been for donkey's horses.'

Then she repacks her bag and leaves.

The queue is cleared and then, seemingly from nowhere, a Dickensian criminal type is sitting on the seat, facing me. Magwitch, perhaps. Abel's head is shaven. He has a large scabbed cut above his eye and another on his cheek. He speaks slowly, with menace and purpose, explaining he'd like a new card. I ask him if he's sure he has lost his previous one. He tells me that he has. I ask him for his surname. I enter it into the system and it reveals that his account has been suspended. He's been 'debarred'. I read through the message history on his account – verbal aggression, one account of physical threat. Disbarment imposed four months before. I'm aware that he's watching me closely as I read. He barely moves, just watches.

'I'm afraid your account has been suspended,' I tell him.

'Why?'

'I'm afraid you've been barred.'

Abel waits and then says: 'No.'

'No?'

'The ban was for three months.'

I have a vague recollection that bans are usually (but not always) of a limited duration and, if this is the case, then his ban is over. I have no choice but to issue him a new card and reactivate the account. The cost of a replacement card is now £1.50 but he chooses not to pay it. He'll pay it next time, he says, standing. His attention remains fixed on me as he walks away. Eventually, thankfully, he turns and I can no longer see his face.

I seek out a manager and explain the transaction to him. He checks the man's card and agrees that the ban has now lapsed. A message is attached to his account explaining this, but alerting the staff to the man's history.

The second challenging customer of the day arrives when I am serving a woman at the main counter – she is sitting in the seat at the desk and all is proceeding smoothly when a figure looms noisily towards us. The figure has become noticeable because of the conversation she is having with herself. She needs a seat and she needs it now. Now! I turn my attention briefly away from the woman I'm serving and see what appears to be a large woman wearing an XXL T-shirt (a marine conservation charity), a skirt, a pair of trainers and a shiny black wig – similar to those Beatle wigs that used to be sold in the early 1960s.

This is Lurching Betty. We've met before on a number of unrewarding occasions. Betty is a tricky one to categorise. First is the issue of gender. She is, to some extent, male. By this I mean she wears predominantly men's clothes, has a man's voice and looks like a man, except for a couple of things. She wears bright red lipstick and has enormous, unfettered breasts which swing freely and extend to just above her waistband. I assume that she is undergoing a gender reassignment and so would prefer to be related to and addressed as a female. Physically, she brings to mind John McCririck, fully blinged.

The second issue is that of her mobility. She is disabled and this is signalled by the fact that she rattles along behind a wheeled, Zimmer-like device with handbrakes and a couple of Formula 1 stickers on the handlebars. The Zimmer contraption is blue. When Betty arrives at the library she has a tendency to lurch to the front of the queue, using the disablement issue to get her there. And when she begins a conversation you know you're in for a long, woeful discussion of the miseries of her life in general, and the more specific trials of her three-mile walk to the library.

Today, she needs a seat and she needs it now (now!). She's at my customer's shoulder and is sweating profusely and shaking with what she tells us is exhaustion. The customer gives way and stands, and Betty slumps into the chair, parking her walking device next to it. I continue serving the customer but Betty begins a conversation with me, ignoring the woman I'm serving.

'Just walked here. Three miles . . .' She begins an account of her epic journey from home, through town, to the library. I try and break in, explaining that I'm actually in the process of serving somebody, but Betty presses on, undeterred.

I finish serving the woman, who, by dint of a great force of will, has managed to keep her temper. She snaps a terse 'Thank you' and leaves, and I now have no choice but to deal with Betty. I remember a Radio 4 polemic about sexual orientation in which the reader discussed gender reassignment and told the story of his son's experiences at a university in America where gender was the latest hot issue. One of the students, in the midst of a sex change, refused to accept the definition of either male or female. The preferred tag was 'they' so perhaps the definition will catch on.

'I was on the radio last night,' Betty offered. 'Speaking to a man in Philadelphia. That's why I'm tired.'

Betty relates the content of her dull, late-night conversation and then goes on and on about something else.

Ten minutes later she leaves, having neither taken out nor returned a book. The important thing, she confides, is that now she has sat down for fifteen or so minutes she can embark on her epic journey home.

Later that day another of the noisy regulars arrives. Barry has few teeth. He's tall and huge and very loud. Today, he's wearing shorts. The legs on display are swollen massively and very red. Barry always remains standing when being served – he prefers to broadcast the conversation to the entire ground floor of the library. Even those upstairs can hear it.

'Not got my ticket. My name's Simpson.'

I look up his name.

'NOW,' he begins, 'the books are all overdue.' I check and his twelve books (all nonfiction, mainly railway books) are all indeed overdue. 'Just got out of hospital. You'll have to renew them. I've been too busy. I'm suing the consultant. Bloody shambles. SNAFU.'

Something has apparently gone terribly wrong following an operation on his leg, the full details of which are broadcast around the building as well as a brief précis of his former profession, which he mentions every time he is in. Barry then does a handbrake turn into an anecdote about a man called Anthony who is thirty-five but who calls Barry 'Dad'. This is offered as being beyond ridiculous, but Barry is probably in his sixties so could feasibly have fathered Anthony. Whether he has or not, Barry takes a paternal role because Anthony's parents (millionaires, apparently) have abandoned him and he is an alcoholic who was routinely 'doing ninety units' a day. He's now 'down to five' but apparently you can't drop your intake that rapidly without serious consequences – physical and mental, so Barry is helping Anthony deal with the consequences.

The final turn in the conversation leads to a brief portrait of Anthony's mother who is 'an habitual turps-nudger', but is now 'off the juice entirely' after receiving a year of intense counselling. However, this has somehow turned her into a 'serial shagger' – so Anthony doesn't get a look in.

The ground-floor staff and customers are now fully up to date with Barry's life story. He needs 'a slash' and sets off for the Gents on painful legs. His place is taken by a middle-aged man in a leather jacket, borrowing the *Withnail and I* DVD. A kindred spirit. He is also taking out a number of CDs – a new Boz Scaggs album (we both agree that we thought he was dead) and *Katy Lied* by Steely Dan. A man after my own heart.

But I am sweating and red-faced. I have nearly finished issuing the CDs when I hear Barry behind me – behind the desk.

'Word of advice,' he calls to all within a half-mile radius. 'Cold water on the neck and on the wrists. Brings down your body temperature immediately.'

I thank him and thankfully he has nothing more to say.

The leather-jacketed man says he also has some advice to offer. I tell him I'm in the market for advice today. 'Never pet a burning dog,' he says, concluding the transaction.

His advice stays with me.

Mid-afternoon, during a quiet moment upstairs in Nonfiction, I Google 'Never pet a burning dog': 5,605,000 results are returned. A respondent to Yahoo suggests the origins:

> I'm thinking you're asking this because of the recent 'Generation Kill' episode on HBO, correct? The saying, 'Never pet a burning dog,' is indicated because the characters had thought they were extending what they believed to be a helping hand to the oppressed people, but now see the ramifications of doing so are poor, and finding that the good they thought they were doing is in question, and the likelihood of harm befalling them for their efforts is greater than ever because of the influx of young Arab men from outside Iraq wanting to fight westerners.

The phrase has also been used by an American band called douBt ('heavy rock riffs to cosmic grooves') as the title of their debut album.

I make a mental note to check out both Generation Kill and douBt when I get home.

Dog Days

Walking past the AstroTurf greensward on the way in to work the day begins with a sharp, high-pitched scream. An unwary young woman on her mobile has just lost her breakfast bacon bap to the first seagull raid of the day. Her cry prompts the gull to drop the bap. It backs off, head raised, shouting as loudly as she did. A young language student waiting for the library to open raises himself from one of the deckchairs Facilities have just put out and returns the bap to the shaken woman.

One of the first customers to the desk is a white-haired woman in her eighties. She looks weary, defeated. She puts her James Patterson books down on the desk and sighs.

'They're all overdue,' she says, with the air of someone who has not transgressed this way before – but somehow she no longer cares.

I return the books. All have a small overdue charge.

'I've lost the will to live,' she says. This is not delivered in the usual jokey way of the office worker peering helplessly at a frozen computer. This is the full Samuel Beckett no future, pointlessness of life scenario.

'I'm sorry,' I prompt.

'My dog died. Monday. I had to have her put down.' Her eyes tear, but she holds them in check. She is a strong woman, unused to displaying her emotions in public. 'She's been with me since I retired. Civil Service. And now I still wait to hear her footsteps in the morning. Awful.'

'I'm sorry,' I say again.

'Ridiculous. It's not a person. It's an animal.'

I offer some platitude about the relationship between people and their pets. She smiles. She might replace the dog – one day. But it's too soon.

I waive the overdue fines on the grounds of 'illness', which I think is justifiable. She thanks me and she leaves.

It's the first week of the schools' summer break and a father is striding rapidly towards the door with his daughter trailing several steps behind. From the look of it, it's his first day off too. He pats his breast pocket. 'Keys, check.' He consults a list on a scrap of paper. 'Post office, check. Come on, Samantha – keep up!' Samantha doubles her pace.

'Bank. Check . . .'

The list slowly fades out as he leaves the library, Samantha in hot pursuit.

It's Wednesday and Trish is in and talking animatedly to some-body. I stand up to see who she's chatting to but she's alone and her conversation is being conducted with a carousel of DVDs. 'Oh yeah, I remember the Beatles . . .' Her monologue goes on but she has dropped her voice and I can no longer hear her.

She turns and sees me. 'Oh, 'ello,'

'Hello, Trish.'

'I know you, don' I?' (See previous conversation: Married? Darren? No. Name? He in? Not today. He married?)

She's wearing a pink baseball cap with a wide brim, pink shoes with sparkles on the Velcro straps, pink sweatshirt and an orange hi-vis jacket.

'I'm not married,' she tells me.

'No?'

'No.'

'Boyfriend?'

'No. Don't want to get married. Too expensive, I've decided. Do you like coffee?'

'Yes.'

'I like coffee. Nice coffee here. Milk. Do you like coffee with milk?'

'Yes.'

'We didn't come last week. Had the week off.'

'Yes, I know.'

'Bye-bye.'

'Bye, Trish.'

A young man with severe learning difficulties approaches the counter with his carer. His face is scar-pitted and unshaven. His teeth protrude, he is thin and is wearing a red sweatshirt. His valuables are in a transparent pouch, which is attached to him by a thin chain around his neck. When he speaks, he directs his conversation towards the floor – refusing to meet my eye. His carer is a thin East European woman in light blue East European denims – mid-thirties with bleached blonde hair – a tough-faced woman with a perpetual half smile, perhaps a sneer. The man is returning a child's DVD – Disney's *Aladdin*. I take it from him. He says something, but I can't understand it. I ask him to repeat it, but his language is impenetrable.

His carer tells me he would like to renew the DVD. I ask for his card, but he has lost it – I ask for his name.

'Goofy,' he says clearly. His first audible word: 'Goofy.'

I smile. 'Goofy?'

The carer's smile is turned off. 'No, David,' she says – with a degree of harshness. 'Not your nickname. Your real name.'

'Goofy,' David says, smiling at me.

By the carer's response, by her sudden change in attitude, I know that the name has been awarded to him: earned by his looks and his inability to communicate: Goofy. The carer gives me David's surname. I renew the DVD and Goofy is hurriedly removed and taken back to his care home. Trish, at that moment, passes the counter. She holds up her large cup of cappuccino and smiles. I picture the circumstances in which David lives, imagining the belittlement, and I know that Trish's sanctuary is quite different. I hope that my suspicions about David's world are wrong.

Happy Returns

Torrential rain has caused a leak in the skylights and water is dripping from some fifty feet up onto the PCs on the ground floor. Trev has found a black bin liner and has shrouded one PC in it but the summer rain is so intense that the customer sitting to the left of it is now also being rained on. Trev is summoned again and informs us that the remedy is that they will shove the table of PCs away from the leak when the library is closed.

At the staff briefing it's reported that some libraries are now experimenting with 'dynamic stock'. This means that books no longer have a permanent home but will float around the community libraries in the area, being lodged wherever they are returned. This, it is anticipated, will reduce the need for the green Van Box system of shipping books around the county – and save subsequent processing time. At this morning's briefing, the issue of 'floaters' was discussed, although the term was immediately flagged up by one staff member as needing some work.

The summer holidays plus the rain guarantees that the library will be full. The staffing levels today, however, are high, which means that the surplus is expected to clear the backlog of shelving. Depending on mood this is either mind-numbingly boring or strangely compelling – the challenge being to clear the returns shelves before the hour is up.

Fiction shelving is relatively straightforward. Books are arranged, of course, by the first letter of surname. There are a few qualifiers to this. Short-story collections, if by a single author, belong with the author's other books. Collections by more than one author are shelved by the first letter of the anthology title. Where an author's name is double-barrelled their books are to be found under the initial letter of the second surname, treating the first surname as a middle name unless this is hyphenated, in which case they belong beside those sharing the first letter of the first of the hyphenated names (i.e. Grace Wynne-Jones is shelved under W for Wynne, not J for Jones). The 'Mcs' and 'Macs' are treated as a separate sequence at the beginning of the Ms before any surnames beginning with Ma. Surnames beginning with de or du are shelved under D, rather than by the second part of the name, thus Louis de Bernières belongs under Deb rather than at B for Bernières and Daphne Du Maurier is shelved under Dum. Authors with surnames beginning with O' are shelved in the relevant part of the O run, i.e. O'Reilly would be shelved after Ore and before Oreland. The fiction stock is no longer subdivided into general fiction, horror, romance, science fiction and crime. Crime remains the only fiction subdivision although spines of the earlier subdivisions still carry their coloured square denoting the genre.

Shop-floor library staff fall into one of two categories: the sitters or the shelvers. The sitters spend each hour at their workstations attending to customers and, when there are no customers to be served, read their emails or surf the net. The shelvers are rarely seated. At each workstation is a trolley laden with returned books. The shelvers are averse to seeing full trolleys and spend their time piloting the trolley up and down the aisles, depositing these books back to the shelves.

There are two methods of doing this and, again, library staff tend to fall into one of two camps. The first camp adopts the method of surveying the returned books and then grabbing an armful of authors with the same initial letter of surname. The teetering pile is then distributed in the relevant section. The second camp favours an initially more time-consuming but ultimately more time-effective method. This involves putting all of the books on the trolley in alphabetical order and then wheeling it round from A to Z, getting rid of the entire backlog in one journey. Today, I have adopted method B and seem to have a disproportionately large number of copies of *Fifty Shades of Grey*.

The nation's brief flirtation with middlebrow pornography was, I thought, over. The nation's fastest-selling paperback ever had, by 2015, reached global sales of around 150 million, spawned a movie and earned a ban in libraries in at least three states of America as well as parts of Brazil. We've also now seen the second wave, i.e. the hilarious spin-offs: *Fifty Sheds of Grey*, *Fifty Shades of Oy Vey* and even cookbooks – including the less successfully resonant *Fifty Shades of Chicken*. At the time of writing there are currently ninety-eight spin-offs listed on one of the booklover's websites. My favourite is a cookbook, *Fifty Shades of Gravy*.

But now, it seems, the nation's libido has returned to low light and middle-aged men can, according to one caller to a radio phone-in, emerge from their sheds without being called on to do their duty by their rampant wives. I have, however, issued the *Fifty Shades* audiobook a number of times over the past couple of months to the more elderly customers – always women, on one occasion the eighty-odd-year-old borrower was accompanied by her shocked late-middle-aged son.

But when a book hits the zeitgeist it can have bizarre consequences. When the *Fifty Shades* phenomenon was at its peak, I went into the local art shop to buy some paint. Ahead of me in the queue was an artist looking for an A3 sheet of grey card. The woman behind the counter said that they'd nearly run out – in fact in her entire career she'd never sold so many sheets of grey card and the only thing to which she could put it down was the book and film.

The way books are chosen by borrowers is often unpredictable. There are two schools of thought among longstanding library staff. Putting aside the books that are garnering huge review coverage or have somehow miraculously become word-of-mouth hits, one school of thought holds that readers 'graze', i.e. they don't know what they want and tend to wander along the aisles looking for a spine that catches their attention. Some customers regularly visit the 'recently returned' stand on the assumption that if someone else has returned a book then it must have some intrinsic merit. The second school of thought holds the more conventional view that readers visit the library in search of a particular book. If a copy is not available then a reservation is made (at a cost of £1). The current pro-libraries lobby subscribe to the first school, arguing that a grazing customer is more likely to choose to chew on something of more 'quality' if the stock has been curated by a stock buyer who knows his or her literature, rather than a wholesaler whose prime motivation is profit.

Colour Supplement

The 'How do readers choose books?' debate has taken an unexpected turn. A week ago, somebody had the bright idea of unearthing every yellow-jacketed book that they could find and displaying them all on a stand by the entrance. It did, we had to admit, look quite striking despite the fact that the only thing that unified these books was the colour of the packaging. The assumption among the old-timers was that they would gather dust on the stand for a couple of weeks and then somebody would come up with some other marketing wheeze and the yellow books would go back on the shelves. It soon became apparent, however, that the yellow promotion was the most successful the library had ever mounted – books were being taken at an alarming rate, and soon the number of yellow-jacketed books in the library had diminished to two or three. What this says about the reading public is tricky to analyse – marketing experts will, I'm sure, have their theories, but it does suggest that the grazing school of thought is currently in the ascendancy and perhaps publishers should take this into account when launching new books into the marketplace.

When a customer can't find a book that the catalogue suggests should be on the shelf – 'available' – this radical marketing policy causes a problem for the staff. Faced with the challenge of a missing book, the library officer takes a number of steps. The first is to re-check the shelf, apologising to the customer for not believing them, but suggesting that books often aren't exactly where they are supposed to be. If the customer is proved right and the book is not there then it's useful practice to check on the computer system when it was last borrowed. If it was borrowed more than a couple of years ago, the chances are it has been 'lost' (nicked). If it was returned in the previous forty-eight hours, it's likely to be on one of the returns shelves or trolleys or could be in transit from another library on its way back home. It might, however, be on the 'recently returned' carousel. If it's not there, it could be on the 'Summer Reads' stand, or possibly the 'Shades of Black' promotion, or perhaps one of the other promotions currently running ('Modern Classics', for example). The yellow carousel is the last port of call. Yesterday, after trying all of the other options, I discovered an Isaac Asimov hiding there, much to the customer's delight.

At the morning briefing at which this is discussed, one of the senior staff members relates that when she was working in her previous library, at Christmas they gift-wrapped a number of books and left them under a Christmas tree. Customers were invited to take a chance on a wrapped book and it proved very popular.

The summer reading scheme here has now been running in Children's for three weeks. During the school holiday young readers are encouraged to choose six books and write a short review of each one. This earns them stickers and medals for their achievements. Each participant begins by choosing one of eight cartoon figures as their avatar. On the small sheet of paper with the cartoon on it, the child's name, age and favourite author are written and the paper is pinned onto a noticeboard. As the challenge progresses the cartoon is moved to the next noticeboard and then, ultimately, to the finishing board.

Not long before the library closes, a tall black woman and her eager five-year-old daughter arrive at the desk and the mother asks if her daughter can join the scheme. I begin the process of enrolment by asking the child to pick her avatar. Six of the eight are Caucasian, two are not. The girl chooses a Caucasian figure to represent her. Her mother points to the non-Caucasian girl on the board, but the girl says she is happy with her choice and her mother accepts it, slightly perturbed.

In Children's, crayons are provided for the younger members to scrawl pictures on the pieces of scrap paper left around for them on the low tables. In their enthusiasm the image often spills beyond the boundaries of the paper and onto the table, leaving a perfect white rectangle on the surface bordered in spidery colours. Today, a child was, I think, attempting a self-portrait. The dress was rendered in the colour of the one she was wearing and the hair of the image was long and fair. The girl was Caucasian, denoted by the bright red crayon she was using for her face.

I mention this only because I have just been reading a book about the experiences of a library assistant in California in the 1990s. Don Borchert reported that it was not acceptable to wish people 'Happy Christmas' in December. Given the racial and religious diversity of the country, it was safest to bid them a 'happy holiday'. This cautiousness reached new heights when his library was obliged to purchase ('at almost government contract-like expense') something called 'multicultural crayons'. Apparently, 'there are more a dozen of them per box, and each marker has been designed to more assiduously resemble different racial tones'.[8] Given the budgetary limitations of the library here it seems unlikely that this will be replicated.

Due to funding constraints the number of timesheets printed each morning is now only four rather than six. When the current paper stocks run out there's a question mark over whether we will be able to order more. The staff printers are now being replenished with thin, yellowing, recycled paper. This was trialled for a while in the public printers until those using the facility complained that their job prospects would be hampered if they supplied their CVs on what looked like used toilet paper. It's hard to explain to a customer why there is simply no paper for their child to colour in – but there isn't. Cuts.

And one customer has got wind of an alleged absurdity over the public donations boxes (labelled 'Help fund your libraries future!'). These glass-fronted vessels usually have a few coppers and buttons in them. The rumour is that they were hand-built and cost several hundred pounds, probably bringing them into profit by the century's end. The customer is planning a Freedom of Information request to find out the exact sums spent.

It's been a long day, 8.30 a.m. until 7 p.m., and my patience is frayed as the shift finishes. Thankfully the rain has stopped.

As I leave the library I spot Lurching Betty. She's not been in to the library for a while and I've never seen her out in the evening so it's a surprise to encounter her. She seems to have added another disablement to her armoury. Hanging from a strap on her right wrist is now a white stick. I have not encountered Lurching Betty since she tragically lost her sight but I'm glad to see it hasn't affected her mobility – she is walking rapidly behind her tripod device. But then, contrary to the evidence of the white stick, I see her spot a hairdresser's A-frame which has been moved from its usual place, tight against the shop front, to the centre of the narrow pavement, blocking easy passage. Betty aims squarely at the A-frame and hits it. She then falls to the floor, moaning loudly, attracting the attention of three young female students, loitering after leaving the library. They immediately dash across the street and ask her if she's all right.

'I'm not, actually,' Lurching Betty informs them. They offer to help. I leave them to it as they try to get her back to her feet.

Bookmark 3

A brown parcel tag (quite new) inside a paperback copy of
Lord of the Flies. In black fountain-pen ink, in slightly untidy
writing, is written:

In meeting and sharing with him whilst travelling in SE
Asia, years later we met up again and through our con-
versations I joined VSO and worked for three years in
TZ. That changed my life. X.

The Pumpkin Polisher

Shortly after opening I catch a brief snatch of a conversation. Two men are talking. Both are fit-looking, early sixties, wearing Pringle sweaters and slacks. They have called in on their way to playing golf. One says: 'Yeah, she said goodnight and that's the last thing she said. In the morning she was cold.' I don't hear the response.

A more cheerful character visits the desk later in the morning. He has a full head of grey hair, a light leather jacket, darkened around the collar, and eyes that express huge delight with the way the world has treated him. He has come to retrieve his walking stick, which he left there an hour or so before.

'Sometimes I forget I can't walk very well without a stick,' he tells me, 'so I put it down and forget it. And then my leg hurts and I remember I need it – and then I try and remember where I've left it. Forget my head if it wasn't screwed on,' he says, laughing.

His breath is unusual – not unpleasant, but carrying a citrus fragrance.

'My daughters bought me two sticks,' he says. 'Lost them both.'

The man is eightyish years old. He comes in regularly for his crime fiction. He's mobile but his mobility is declining and his world is closing in. He's often looking for a brief chat in the quiet hour after opening and a book he's read about in the Sundays. From previous conversations I know that he spent his life as a picture framer in London and retired at sixty: 'I wanted to travel while I still had the health and the nerve. You need nerve to travel . . . I can't travel now, so I'm glad I did it when I could.'

He's been all over the world.

'For a few years,' he tells me today, 'I had two camper vans. One in Europe, one in Florida, and I'd travel between them with my partner. We went across the States five times over ten years. Small-town America, mainly. I liked meeting people. The Americans didn't travel – they thought England was a small country and I'd know everybody . . . "Do you know so and so? He lives in Worcestershire." It was terrific. Lots of adventures. One day I go round the back of the van for a piss. This is in the Everglades. I turn round and there's fifteen or so alligators looking at me. I run back in the van. It's all about nerve. One night I went to Central Park in New York. Two fat coppers are standing there. They say, "Where you going?" I say, "I'm going in the park." They say, "Not if you want to come out again." I miss travelling. Yes, I miss it.'

'Is your partner still alive?'

'No . . . No. But I'm lucky. My two daughters, they look after me.'

We've been talking for ten minutes. Unlike some of the other customers, he knows the limit and, taking a cue from a pause, tells me to have a good day and leaves.

When it comes to enquiries, the Travelling Man knows the limits. He asks for a book, perhaps two, but he doesn't tend to use that as a springboard for more information. For that reason,

I'm always glad to serve him. Ask anyone involved in dealing with the public and they will tell you that one of their most profoundly annoying characteristics is that if there is somebody around to answer a question then they will find a question to ask – often one thought up on the spur of the moment. The library is, of course, recognised as one of the few places in a town or city where information is dispensed free of charge but it takes a while for the new library officer to discover where to find it. Where, for example, is the section on copyright law? Where do we keep *Debrett's* or *The International Who's Who*? Do we have access to Which Online? Ancestry.co.uk? (Yes.) I'm looking for all of the Children's Parliamentary Acts passed in 2004, is there a section I can find them? (Yes.) I'm having an argument with my son, do you have the *OED*, it's the only way I can win? (Yes.) I'm looking for the vocal score for *Peter Grimes*. Do you have it? (Yes.) I'm writing an essay on Rage Against the Machine, do you have any books on them? (Yes, but your classmates have got there before you.) Do you have an Ordnance Survey map for x/y/z? (Yes, we have them all.) I need the *Yellow Pages* for Newcastle. Do you have it? (Yes.) Can you tell me why the West Indians were wearing black armbands in the International 20/20 Cricket final against England? (I suggest, tentatively, that they might have been mourning diminutive anecdotist Ronnie Corbett, but further investigation revealed it was a trainer.)

Other questions, or queries I have tried to answer recently are:

1. Why are the buses not stopping on North Street?
2. I'm looking for the will of my father, who died forty years ago in Ottawa, how can I do it?

3. Have there been any major developments in CBT [Cognitive Behavioural Therapy] over the past five or six years?
4. Can you recommend a bed and breakfast?
5. Can you let me have the postal address of the Home Secretary?
6. Do you know what the weather forecast is for tomorrow?
7. Does the 'North West' telephone directory cover Chester?
8. I'm looking for a man who worked with me and my husband twenty-five years ago. Can you help?
9. Do you have an Ordnance Survey map of South America [area unspecified]?
10. Is there an old-fashioned telephone box nearby?
11. Do you have a bubbler? [Further questioning reveals that this is the Australian term for water fountain.]
12. Do you have *The Goldfish* by Donald Tart?
13. Would you mind if I phoned my doctor to check the time of my appointment?
14. Can I send a fax?
15. Is Arthur Scargill alive?
16. Do you have a stapler/pencil sharpener/paper/pen/pencil/ iPhone charger/change for the printer/a spoon/the time/the time in Montreal?

The answers to some enquiries are, of course, found on the shelves of Nonfiction in which books are organised by the Dewey Decimal Classification system (DDC; see the Appendix); this is one of the three major 'universal' schemes, the other two being 'Universal Decimal Classification' and 'Library of Congress Classification'. The DDC bears the name of American Melvil Dewey who, like many before him, recognised that there's no point in having information if you can't find it. This is made more challenging by the fact that, as Alberto Manguel suggests, a library is a constantly evolving entity: 'It multiplies seemingly unaided, it reproduces itself by purchase, theft, borrowings, gifts, by suggesting gaps through association, by demanding completion of sorts.'[9]

Over the centuries, books have been categorised in numerous ways. The earliest schemes organised them alphabetically, broadly by subject. In 1475 the 'custodians' of the Vatican Library (Parmenio and Mammacino) compiled a catalogue. A row of tables ran up each side of the first room:

> to these tables books were chained in subject in great numbers. The catalog follows the layout of the tables: the first table on the left holds books of the Bible; the next table is reserved for the Fathers of The Church; the following tables pass through the Doctors of the church to the works of saints and to canon law and contemporary theological works.[10]

The catalogue was organised alphabetically and new titles were added in the margins. By the eighteenth century the continued growth in the collections rendered the catalogue useless. But, as early as the seventeenth century, Samuel Pepys recognised that numbers rather than the alphabet were more useful for his diaries and he enumerated them for his 'easy finding them to read'.[11] The Paris Bookseller's Classification (1842) developed by Jacques Charles Brunet is generally accepted as the first of the modern book classification systems and in it he broke the stock down into five major categories: theology, jurisprudence, sciences and arts, belles-lettres, and history.

For a system to work, a book, unlike a subject heading where multiple terms can be assigned to each work, can only belong to a single class. If you want to stand any chance of tracking it down it can only be in one place at a time and that place on the shelf (relative to the books around it) has to be the same whichever part of the world you're browsing.

We take the Dewey Decimal Classification system for granted, but the man who gave his name to it, Melvil Dewey, was a driven, complex and apparently unsavoury character. We encountered his influence before in terms of his defining what a library and a librarian should be and perhaps it's worth (while we're upstairs in Nonfiction and the printers are working, and the students are studying quietly and neither Brewer nor Wolf have shown their faces for a while to cause trouble) finding out a little about him. Should you want the unexpurgated story, *Irrepressible Reformer* by Wayne A. Wiegand is the book to read. It's hard to find. There was no copy to be had in this library or in the wider reaches of the inner library empire so I bought a copy on Amazon. A stamp inside the front cover suggests its last home was the 'Margaret D. Sneddon Library, Davenport College, Grand Rapids, M.I.' Beneath an orange barcode on the spine, it still has its original Dewey classification number: 020.92.

Melville Louis Kossuth Dewey (he truncated his first name later) was the second son of Joel and Eliza Greene Dewey, born in Jefferson County in 1851. Wave after wave of evangelism and reform had swept the district in the first half of the nineteenth century, leading historian Whitney Cross to label it the 'Burned-Over District'. Dewey's evangelical parents, shopkeepers, were part of the growing middle class and, as he recalled, 'famous . . . for being the hardest working in town'. Both taught stoicism and preached humility. 'Praise to the face is an open disgrace,' Eliza often told her son.

Even as a teenager, Dewey was concerned for his future, determined to 'leave the world better than I found it'. One night he settled on 'reform' as his life's work and, next day, bought a pair of cufflinks with the letter 'R' as a constant reminder. But the biggest indication of his future career path is to be found in his 'Table of Accounts', which he began at the age of fifteen and listed his height, weight, clothing, assets and 'insolvency'. In ten years he went from 5 feet 5 and a quarter inches, 120 pounds and $125 in assets, to 5 feet 11 and a half inches, 174 pounds and no assets.

While a university student he founded the Library Bureau, which sold index cards and filing cabinets and established the standard dimensions of catalogue cards. It was after graduating from Amherst College that he was employed to manage the library there and reclassify its collections. He disliked the arbitrary methods used by most libraries by which books were arranged alphabetically but without reference to subject matter and he was determined to devise a better solution. And then: 'one Sunday, during a long sermon . . . the solution flasht over me so that I jumpt in my seat and came very near shouting "Eureka!" Use *decimals* to number a classification of all human knowledge in print.'[12]

The scheme he submitted to the Amherst College Library committee in May 1873 was constructed on the premise that knowledge could be divided into nine main classes (the final 'first summary' was actually divided into ten classifications). Each of the classes could be further subdivided by adding a decimal. Further subclasses could be added by assigning a second digit. The system was therefore infinite so long as the main classes were robust and all-encompassing. In defining these, he sought the help of William Torrey Harris, an educator, lexicographer and St Louis school superintendent. Harris' idea was that books should be arranged alphabetically under subject, so that they had a relative rather than a fixed location. In the St Louis libraries, Harris had already divided knowledge into nine major classes, built on two platforms:

> (1) ideas of Sir Francis Bacon, who had argued that the three faculties of the human mind – memory, imagination and reason – produced three categories of learning – history, poetry and philosophy, each of which could be further subdivided; and (2) the ideas of F. W. Hegel, who inverted Bacon's order to give a more prominent role to philosophy, from which the rest of the structure follows. From philosophy, Harris saw a natural structure of knowledge progressing to theology, government, philology, nature, the useful and the fine arts, and finally, geography, biography and history.[13]

Dewey had his supporters and detractors. He was apparently hard to like. Wiegand notes his 'old nemesis—a persistent inability to control himself around women' as a chronic cause of trouble on the job. When Dewey opened his School of Library Economy at Columbia College to women he asked for a photograph on the grounds that 'you cannot polish a pumpkin'. Advances towards a number of women on a 1905 American Library Association (ALA) trip to Alaska led to him being ostracised by the organisation.[14] Two members threatened they would resign from the ALA if Dewey did not stop. But it was his involvement with the Lake Placid Club development that, in

1904, led to a petition being delivered to the New York State Board of Regents demanding his removal as State Librarian. The Lake Placid Club, a model community of cottages and clubs in a private park, had a policy of excluding Jews and other religious and ethnic groups. Although he was never eager to publicise the fact, Dewey and his wife Annie had written the original club rules. The Regents declined to remove Dewey but issued a public rebuke, and in the summer of 1905 he resigned as a result.

The DDC is active and still evolving and now used in more than 135 countries. As its parent website now boasts:

> The Dewey editorial office is located in the Decimal Classification Division of the Library of Congress, where classification specialists annually assign over 110,000 DDC numbers to records for works cataloged by the Library . . . The editors prepare proposed schedule revisions and expansions and forward the proposals to the Dewey Decimal Classification Editorial Policy Committee (EPC) for review and recommended action.

The enquiries desk no longer exists in this library. The staff in Nonfiction attempt to service the numerous enquiries and there's a dedicated staff member who can be radioed in the event of a complex query, but the dedicated, long-serving experts have gone and been replaced by generalists doing their best along the avenues of shelves using a map devised by the flawed reformer Melvil Dewey.

Bookmark 4

Laminated:

Dear Ella [smiley face]
You have worked so hard in Year 3 and been such great company. See you in Year 4.
Love from Mrs Belham

Work/life Balance

Nonfiction again. Afternoon. The summer is drawing to a close and the penchant for staff wearing shorts has tailed off. Only one hardy soul clings on to his combat shorts. Rain is streaking down the tall windows of the upper floor and customers troop in with rain-specked coats and weary faces. The long room to the side of Nonfiction on the upper floor is full of students studying quietly. There's an air of intense concentration. I wander through, picking up litter, empty coffee cups and a few discarded books, and count the number of students in the room: sixty-eight and not a spare chair. I wonder where they'd be if they didn't have the library in which to study.

I return to the desk when I spot a man, mid-sixties, arriving there. He has a suntanned face. He's lean, fit-looking, and he wants to talk. You can always tell when customers want a chat because they approach the desk without urgency, an immediate question or concern or a book to be issued or returned.

'Hello. How can I help you?' I ask him.

'Oh, hello.' His voice is cultured – he seems surprised that somebody has arrived to help him – as if he would have been happy to wait at the desk all day. 'I'm looking for educational courses. I don't know if you can help.'

As we are taught – define the parameters, identify the issue.

In a role-play session during training we were asked to respond to this query: 'Do you have a book on China?' The trainees all assumed the customer was going on holiday – the trainer revealed that the customer was actually a collector of ceramics. A few well-judged questions make a search more effective. The other lesson the trainer was keen to promote was not to make assumptions. It's easy to fall foul of this one. The first time it happened to me was when a middle-aged man and woman arrived at the desk with ten or eleven hardback crime novels. The woman handed over a library card. In issuing the books I saw that the card belonged not to her but to a young adult. I joshingly suggested that the couple should encourage their son to visit the library himself – be good for him to get out and get some exercise. The woman looked at the man. It was left to him to tell me that their son was housebound, and had been for the past year. There was no anger, but there was a weariness about him. I apologised.

'Are you looking for a course to take?' I asked the suntanned senior.

'No, I'm a tutor.'

'So you're looking to teach?'

'Yes. Part-time. I'm retired. Just. Well, two months ago and I need something to do.'

The man – Mr McKenzie – tells me he has spent his life teaching economics. He started his teaching life locally but then took the opportunity to go to the United Arab Emirates to teach there. He kept a house locally but spent ten months a year in the Arabian Peninsula. He taught the equivalent of O and A levels, mainly to the children of ex-pats, but now he is at a loose end.

'I'm not married,' he tells me. 'And . . . frankly I'm bored to death.'

Living so long out of the country he has no network of friends. He has no children, no hobbies or interests beyond the news. He watches CNN or BBC News all the time.

'Late afternoons are the worst. I feel like I'm peering into an infinity of nothingness. There's nothing ahead. No point.'

I sympathise. I took redundancy two years ago from the day job and the first year was unsettling. Routine runs deep.

An internet search throws up a number of local agencies that employ freelance tutors. It surprises Mr McKenzie. The standard of education nowadays, he says, is declining. He worries for the world but he leaves the library with a lighter step.

The longer you work in the library the more you come to recognise those who seem to play a smaller part. A constant presence but who choose not to draw attention to themselves: the extras.

One such man arrives each day but it's only after a few weeks that I begin to notice him. He's always dressed smartly, as if for work. He wears a sand-coloured jacket, brown trousers, white shirt and red tie. Whatever the weather he has a light, fawn mac over his arm. He is almost totally bald. His head shines under the lights. The defining feature of his face is his nose, which is long and pointed. His eyes are blue. He is probably in his mid- to late-sixties and his neutral expression doesn't invite conversation. Each day he comes at around 10.30 and stays until the mid-afternoon. While he's here he reads the *Daily Telegraph* from cover to cover, unhurriedly. When he has finished he re-folds the paper and returns it to the shelf. This is rare. Most customers, having finished with the papers, tend to discard them in a chaotic pile on one of the low tables, leaving the reassembly for the staff to do. They seem to assume that nobody else will be interested in the paper they've just read.

When the tidy, mac-carrying gent leaves, he does so courteously, as if he's leaving a hotel in which he's taken permanent residence, catching the eye of a member of staff and nodding a thank you.

I imagine he's retired. But I also suspect, like many retirees, he misses the routine of work and has replaced his work hours with visits to the library. This might sound fanciful, but last Monday he arrived not in his usual suit and tie, but in a casual short-sleeved shirt, open-toed sandals and light chinos. He did the same the following day and the next and the next. This Monday he was back in his formal attire. I can only assume that for a week he was on holiday and had dressed accordingly, but had now returned to work.

AUTUMN

Sindy Incidentally

Autumn has officially arrived, marked not by the leaves copper-ing the pavements or the mint in the garden turning to twigs, but by the removal of the AstroTurf on the piazza and the pack-ing up of the ping-pong tables.

As mentioned before, libraries like to keep things simple – perhaps to leave no room for confusion. Being surrounded by millions of words promotes caution. One of the first jobs of the day, pre-opening, is to empty the Silver Bin. As its name suggests it's silver (ish) and it is . . . well, nearly a bin. The Silver Bin is the repository of the books returned when the library is shut. The letterbox is enormous. In the morning the bin is approached with caution, especially when the weather is inclement because the books inside it tend to be damp, occasionally saturated. This is not the fault of the bin itself but of the customers returning the books. Sometimes they are in a plastic bag, but usually not. Other items are occasionally posted through the letterbox: over the past few months I have found a training shoe in there, an empty egg box and an unopened can of Stella Artois.

I have yet to find anything animate in there (bar a couple of spiders) unlike Vicki Myron, head librarian in Spencer, Iowa. One winter's morning she discovered a tiny kitten almost frozen to death in the drop box. The cat, which she named Dewey, was apparently soon entertaining the locals with his zany antics. As his fame grew, people drove hundreds of miles to meet him and his heart-warming story, *Dewey the Library Cat: A True Story*, can now be found on the library shelves.

At 9.45 a man arrives on the piazza, stares in and points to his watch – indicating that we should be open. We open at ten but he repeatedly gesticulates towards the watch, trying to catch the eye of one of the members of staff wearily setting up the ground floor. When the doors open *Sons of Anarchy* Alan is first in, closely followed by the gesticulating man. Alan has been asked to bring in his DVDs for renewal. I renew his DVDs. He has four seasons of *Sons of Anarchy*, each of which he has had out seven times. I ask him why he likes them.

'They're the best. My boys.'

'Great.'

'Getting a tattoo.'

'Tattoo. You are?'

'Three. On my back, on my arms. My boys.' He jacks a thumb over his shoulder.

'OK. Come and show us when you've had them done.'

'Yeah.'

The only incident of note during the morning is the visit of a well-read thief. The magazines *Private Eye*, *Empire* and the *Spectator* regularly go missing so the current issue of each is kept in a box folder behind the counter. If a customer wishes to read one of them, they have to be signed out. This week's *Private Eye* is requested by a middle-aged man in a flowery shirt and a denim jacket, his reading glasses hanging loose from a leather strap against his chest. As the man signs the sheet, the library officer turns away. When he turns back the folder is gone – stolen not by the man with the *Private Eye*, but by a very quick thief. Facilities are alerted and the CCTV footage is investigated.

At lunch, in the staff tearoom, Trev is loudly warning the staff away from one of the city's notoriously violent transvestites, who has been spotted in the vicinity. Trev and he go back a long way. In fact, Trev knew him when he went under the name Barry. Barry was a quiet but violent soul with many enemies. His fuse was short and he was a gossip. Barry is now known as Sindy and markets himself as a 'Pre-op' in many of the telephone kiosks around the city. He's much in demand because he offers 'full services' and was recently seen by Trev hoiking an unfortunate man out of a phone box by his collar so he could put up his business card. He's tall – over six foot – wears long, flowing ball gowns, a long chestnut wig, and has very white teeth. Trev concludes his warning by telling the assembled staff where Sindy lives, and explains that if anybody is in the market for his services, he has a maid who takes phone bookings.

It's a warm day – a day of autumn sun – so, after my sandwich, I take a walk around the block. As I leave the library, a hen party in pink T-shirts and pink tasselled cowgirl hats crocodile past. They are following a dwarf naked to the waist – his face and muscular torso are painted Incredible Hulk green and he is carrying a huge blow-up phallus that is pointing the way. The women are ranged neatly in height and size behind him – those at the front are shorter, wider and larger than the younger ones at the back. They look like a clip from Jacob Bronowski's *Ascent of Man* TV series. It's 'Trish's Wedding' according to the pink T-shirts they're all wearing and the shortest and widest woman, tagged 'Trish's Mam', is leading the noisy crowd past the library. Thankfully they don't divert inside.

I reach my favourite park bench (slightly damp and sheltering several empty cans) and am glad to find it unoccupied. Piano music floats across the shrubbery. The source of it is a man in a zebra suit playing an electric keyboard, busking to the tourists. I take pleasure in the sun and his Richard Clayderman selection before returning for the afternoon shift.

Sitting on Hot Coals

A rare outing to one of the community libraries. One of the first customers of the day is a garrulous woman who explains she has spent the last three hours cleaning her flat because she has a visitor coming that night. Although the visitor will only stay for an hour she felt the need to thoroughly clean the bathroom, lounge and kitchen. She also made a rare foray into the roof space, where she found four boxes she hadn't opened for twenty years dating from a period she spent in the United States.

'I lived in New Jersey in the 1980s,' she says. 'Newark.'

I ask her what she did there.

'I was a nurse and then I got fed up with that so I got a job demonstrating food in supermarkets – cheese and bacon things. I had to cook them up and then serve them to the customers. I always did a bit extra at the end of the day and took it home for our tea.'

It was the era of Reagan. She didn't enjoy the company of the white Americans but felt an affinity with the black population. She pauses, remembering. 'If I sold two packets of the food the customers got a voucher for two hundred free cigarettes: Chesterfields. Can you imagine that happening today?'

I admit that I can't.

A small girl in a school uniform arrives with her mother, who is pushing a sleeping baby in a pushchair. The girl is lively and outgoing. She is taking out a book on the care of hamsters.

'Do you have a hamster?' I ask her.

'No. My sister has a budgie – Blue.'

'A blue budgie?'

'No. That's his name.'

'Is he blue?'

'Yes. But that's not why we called him Blue.'

'Why did you call him Blue?'

'I can't remember. But he's not very well.'

'How can you tell if a budgie is not well?'

'His pooh is sicky.'

'I see.'

'We're taking him to the vet.'

'I hope he's all right.'

An elderly woman then comes in on painful feet. Her black, single-strap sandals are old but very highly polished. She is wearing a violet-coloured coat of the style and colour advertised in the flyers that fall out of middlebrow Sunday newspapers. She has just, she tells me, had her hair done at the precinct. It's lacquered solid and looks like it would shatter if anybody dared touch it. She rests her walking stick against the desk and announces: 'He's at the chemist's.'

I've never encountered the woman or the absent man to whom she's referring.

'Now . . .' She takes three large books out of her voluminous shopping bag and deposits them with some effort on the counter one by one. 'Two are mine. One is his. I'm bringing them back.'

One is a Dennis Lehane crime novel, the others are by Hilary Mantel and Audrey Magee.

144

The sliding doors hiss open. She turns as an elderly man walks in. 'Ah, there you are. Why did it take you so long?' He is walking gingerly, as if on hot coals. His skin is very yellow. He has a full head of grey hair and a smile that flickers on and off like a faulty bulb. He is suffering. He is carrying an un-bagged but boxed tube of Anusol.

'Put it away!' the woman says, grabbing the tube of Anusol and shoving it into her bag. 'Now choose your books.'

The man offers a smile in my direction, briefly raising his caterpillar thick eyebrows, suggesting that he will comply with the order but only on his terms. He is, however, moving too slowly for the woman, who barks: 'Go and choose a book! I don't like you without a book.'

The man makes it to the crime shelves and, as he begins peering at them, the woman calls: 'You like Billingham!'

The man takes a Baldacci from the shelf. 'I don't remember this one.' He is addressing the book, squinting at the blurb over the top of his gold-rimmed glasses. 'No, I don't think I've read this one.' He looks for reassurance towards the woman, who is now at another shelf.

'*Time of Death*, Billingham. Have you read that?' the woman shouts.

'Who?'

'*Time of Death!*'

'Billingham, did you say?'

'Yes.'

'No, he's a bit . . . You know.'

After further consideration the man brings his Baldacci to the counter and asks me to issue it. I do – but the system throws up the fact that he had it out in 2013. I inform him of this. 'Ah,' he says and troops slowly back to the shelf, carrying the book.

'Have you had the new Clive Cussler – *Ghost Ship*?' the woman calls, taking it off the shelf of 'Recent arrivals' and holding it up for him to see.

The man ignores her and pulls another book from the shelf. 'I know this is an old one, but I'm getting desperate,' he says to the shelf.

'Who is he?' she asks him.

'Who?'

'Him.'

'Ah . . .' The man looks at the cover. 'Robert Crais.'

Again he returns to the counter. I attempt to issue the book – the system reveals he's had it out before. 'Sorry,' I say to him. '2014.'

'Oh dear . . . There was somebody I knew who used to write a small R at the right-hand top of the page in pencil,' the man says. 'So he knew he'd . . .'

'Come on!' the woman calls.

'He's dead now, I'm afraid. Nice chap.'

The next two books he tries are by Andrew Cross.

'2013,' I tell him.

'Really?'

'Yes. Afraid so.'

'Here . . .' The woman bustles forward and pushes past him: 'Stuart MacBride – *Close to the Bone*.'

I take it from her and scan the barcode: '2013,' I tell her. The man smiles. The woman does not. She fetches another Stuart MacBride.

'Sorry. 2014.'

Finally, after widening the search parameters to include female authors, the man returns with *The Lost Abbot* by Susanna Gregory and *Watching the Ghosts* by Kate Ellis. Neither has been issued to him before. He is triumphant as they leave, still bickering. The automatic doors slide open.

'Where did you put your cream?' the woman asks him.

'I don't know. I thought I gave it to you . . .'

'No, you didn't give it to me.'

'Didn't I? I thought I did.'

Their voices trail away.

I'm at the main desk of the central library a couple of days later when a young man approaches the counter from behind (the counter is marooned in the centre of the room with a couple of cupboards behind it).

'Er . . .?' I hear.

I turn. 'Yes?'

'There's somebody in the Gents. In the cubicle. He needs some help.'

I thank the man and my mind turns warily to the kind of help that could be required by a customer in the cubicle of a Gents toilet. I leave the desk and tentatively I open the lavatory door. Immediately I'm greeted by an eye-watering smell and a weak voice calling from the cubicle. 'Hello?'

'Hello,' I say. 'Can I help you?'

'I've had an accident.'

'Ah . . . Are you hurt?'

'No, not hurt. I fainted and . . . well, I've run out of lavatory paper.'

'OK. I'll be back.'

This is beyond my area of responsibility – but does personal care fall within the remit of Facilities? I return to the main desk, retrieve my walkie-talkie and call them.

'Facilities returning.' It's Trev.

'Got a problem . . . in the Gents.'

'What kind of problem?'

'Customer in the cubicle. Needs some help – and some more toilet paper.'

A slight pause, then, 'On my way.'

I meet Trev at the lavatory door and follow him in. I don't need to explain the situation because the old man in the cubicle, prompted by Trev's 'OK, sir?', explains. Mid-motion, he fainted and fell sideways from the pan onto the floor. The motion continued unabated. When he came around he was in a state. He'd tried to 'sort himself out' but had run out of paper.

Graciously, Trev tells me he'll deal with it and I return to the counter. Fifteen minutes later Trev arrives to report that he has sorted the 'old boy' out but has failed to find a spare pair of trousers for him in lost property. He reaches for the antiseptic hand gel on the counter. I expect some revulsion to be expressed – but the old boy has been treated in such a way as to preserve his dignity. I see Trev in a new light.

Supertramp

He is wearing a camouflaged Army combat jacket and combat trousers. His hair is cut close to his skull, he has lost one of his front teeth and the surviving one protrudes from beneath his top lip at an angle of around forty-five degrees. His eyes are very blue and his skin is tanned to the colour of leather. He has a large rucksack with him. Neatly strapped to it is a sleeping bag. He introduces himself as Gareth Junior. He's Welsh.

'I'd like to join up if I can,' he says, smiling.

'Sit down.'

He rests his rucksack on the floor and hangs an arm across it as though embracing the shoulders of a huge, much-loved dog. 'Thing is, see, I don't have a permanent residence.'

'That's OK.'

I ask him where he is living.

'Now?'

'Yes. At the moment.'

'In the woods.' He points and names an area of parkland to the north of the city. 'I came down four days ago. I'm on my way to Copenhagen.'

Gareth, a gentle soul, seems to want to talk. I ask him for ID and he provides his passport. It's clean; well looked after. He has a mobile phone number and an email address. He says he wants to use the computers and will, maybe, borrow a book but it depends how long he stays.

'You're a traveller?'

'Yes. Since I was thirteen.'

'Thirteen?'

'I left home at thirteen. Now I'm twenty-four.'

'And you've been on the road since then?'

'Yes, I have.'

Over the past few months I've met many street sleepers, mostly chaotic, needs-must men (exclusively men) who have fallen off the grid, never an old-fashioned supertramp.

'I live in tepees, tents, anywhere. I learned how to make a bender years back.' He tells me that he prefers to live in the mountains and caves. 'When the weather gets really bad I find work as a chef – well, cook. It pays for the bed and breakfast for a few nights. What I do, see, is buy books, cheap. Paperbacks. Dickens. I like Dickens. And when I've read it I pass it on with a message inside.'

'To?'

'To people I meet when I'm travelling.'

'You like the life?'

'I love it. I couldn't do nine to five . . . Need to travel. Don't like a roof over my head.'

I ask him about his family – whether they were alarmed that he left home at thirteen.

'No. Not at all.'

'Really?'

'Honest to God.'

'What does your father do?'

'He's a Hell's Angel.'

'That's his job?'

'Well – it's the way he lives his life.'

Gareth Junior smiles as I hand him his card. He signs it and tells me: 'I'm a member of twenty-three libraries now. I join one everywhere I go. If I can. Do you know anywhere I can wash? Fresh water? Local river?'

I laugh, but he's not joking. I suggest a charity that has showers and facilities to wash clothes. He thanks me. I offer to call them and make sure they're open. He says it's not necessary.

'Can I use the card now?'

'Yes.'

'Thank you. It was nice to meet you.'

'And you.'

Gareth Junior takes a seat at one of the PCs. When I look across again ten minutes later he is gone.

The Lost Boy

A young woman with close-cropped hair in hessian-type clothing and vegetarian sandals rushes to the counter of Children's and explains she has lost her son. She is red-faced and deeply agitated and holds her mobile phone as if she can somehow conjure up an app that will track him down. I ask her for a description. The boy is two years old, he has light brown hair, brown trousers and a blue striped jumper.

'When did you last see him?' I ask her.

'A few minutes ago. Over there.'

She points towards one of the low tables.

I fetch the walkie-talkie from the desk and radio Facilities. Trev answers my call for the lost child and says he is on his way down. The woman waits, pacing nervously. I too am nervous – ten minutes have now passed and the child is not in Children's nor, a search has revealed, is he on the floor of the main library or in the toilets. The chances of him having climbed the two flights of stairs to the first floor are slim, which means that he might have wandered out and onto the street. The street outside is one way and not much used by cars but it's an area busy with pedestrians.

Trev arrives and asks the woman similar questions. He is, however, slightly more reassuring, telling her it's a common occurrence and she should not worry. She tries a smile but it doesn't quite make the distance from her mouth to her eyes. Trev heads for the door, walkie-talkie in hand. The woman asks if she should follow him. He tells her she should wait where she is, so she does. Trev mounts the gentle wheelchair-friendly slope from Children's to the adult section of the library. The woman waits nervously and I begin to tackle the backlog of shelving.

As I kneel to shelve some books on dinosaurs I overhear three women snacking and talking about the births of their babies. They are eating lunch at one of the small circular tables. One of them says: 'Yes, he has a very big head. When he came out, the top was very pointy.'

Another asks: 'Was he the one that was sucked out?'

'No, that was Jake.'

'He has got a very big head, hasn't he, though?'

'Yes, enormous.'

A child comes up and asks if there's 'somewhere she can read books?' I tell her that she can read them anywhere in the library – but there are comfortable seats by the wall. She thanks me and goes to sit by the wall.

Then two teenage female students – foreign language students by the look of their expensive leisurewear and air of health and wealth – arrive in Children's. Between them, holding their hands, is a small boy with a striped jumper. The hessian-dressed boy's mother dashes towards them and snatches her son back.

'We found him outside Pizza Express,' one of the girls tells her in a Scandinavian accent. 'We thought he might have come from here.'

The woman doesn't manage a thank you or, indeed, any gratitude, but Trev and I thank the girls and they leave. The woman turns to Trev with anger and asks him how a two-year-old child could be allowed to wander out of the library without anyone noticing. Trev explains patiently that the assumption was presumably that the child was being accompanied by one of the many people leaving the library that morning. He manages to maintain a civil smile as the woman leaves.

Gregory's Girl

Read any author's early works and you'll usually encounter a soul stripped bare. Chance upon a late career autobiography and you'll find the same writer being much more circumspect. By the time writers have learned the art of camouflage it's too late, the cat is out of the bag. A good writer is a good reader of his or her own work. You can't be one without the other. I've tried hard not to embellish the stories and characters in this book. There are occasions, however, when a writer confronted with an individual can't help but flesh out the backstory.

It happened one chilly morning when a young woman arrived at the lectern and asked for a scrap of paper. I gave one to her but she didn't immediately retreat. Instead, she stood there, paper in hand, looking thoughtful and clearly wanting to talk. The woman was the Sally Hawkins-type you find in late Mike Leigh films. Fragile, thin, cheaply dressed, hair decently but slightly savagely cut, porcelain complexion, cold fingers, slightly out of time. In the film, or the story you are writing about her, you begin to flesh out the details. It seems likely that the woman is not in a relationship. She cycles to her teaching job, waving cheerily to the shopkeepers on the impossibly cheery main street, and she rings her bell to alert the cheery postman not to cross the road. But this is just a front. The woman's smile hides an emptiness she cannot fill – an emptiness she is forced to confront as she demolishes her three or four bottles of cheap red wine each night or, perhaps, engages in a series of destructive one-night stands with strangers.

'Can I help?' I ask the woman – let's call her Laura.

The real story now begins. This is how it unfolds:

'I don't know,' she says. 'Do you have the Electoral Roll?'

I tell her that we do. It's behind the main counter. The library is quiet so I fetch it. The rules governing use of the Electoral Roll are strict and dictate that it cannot leave the sight of the library officer. People are, of course, allowed to read it and take notes but not to photocopy it. The main challenge when using it is to puzzle through the index, which is designed to confuse. As many will know, the roll is arranged in areas and within each area (each of which is accorded a couple of initials and a couple of digits) streets are arranged alphabetically. What most people don't realise is that there is no index of names, therefore if you're searching for a long-lost family member you are unlikely to find them unless you know the street on which they're living.

I heft the heavy, green tome to a nearby table and ask the young woman which street she's looking for. She tells me.

'Who are you looking for?'

'Gregory,' she says and flashes a quick private smile.

'Gregory?'

She offers a surname. I point her to the relevant section and retreat to the lectern, keeping a distant eye on her as she gets on with it. Soon she looks up and across at me. I return to the table.

'No?' I ask her.

'No,' she says, 'I came down from London this morning to look for him, took a bus from the station and then another and got off at B&Q. I thought I was in the right road but I asked around and nobody seemed to know him. Which is odd, because if you knew Gregory, you'd know he would be known by everybody.'

'A friend?'

She laughs. 'Yes. A friend.'

'I'm sorry. Looks like you've had a wasted journey.'

'Not entirely,' she says. 'Thank you for your help.'

She begins to move away towards the main exit but then she stops and returns.

'There's one other thing.'

'Yes?'

'I know he wrote to the local paper when his wife died.'

'Wife?'

Laura looks away. Now, perhaps, I understand what Gregory was to her and what she was to him.

'She died in hospital. It was a long illness . . . and he wrote to the paper to explain how good they'd been to her, and to him.' She pauses, remembering. 'He said he was tired of the NHS getting such a bad press. He told me about the letter but I never looked it up. I suppose it might be on the internet.'

'I suppose so.'

We return to the lectern and I make a search. Remarkably, the letter to the local paper shows on the first page of results.

'This one?' I ask the woman. She leans towards the screen and reads the letter.

'Yes,' she says. 'How clever. That's Gregory.'

The letter narrates the final days of his wife's life. He has written, he suggests, to counter the usual bad news stories about the NHS. His wife (and indeed he) received tenderness and care, for which he will always be grateful. The letter ends with Gregory's address, the street name, not the number.

'Close,' Laura says.

'Close?'

'I was looking for "Road", but it's "Close".'

A local map reveals that unsurprisingly the close is not far from the road. She was in the right vicinity.

'Thank you so much,' she says and offers her hand to shake. 'Back to B&Q.' Her fingers are, indeed, cold.

She leaves in search of Gregory. An ex-boss? A tutor or lecturer? There must be a significant gap in years – twenty or thirty – but perhaps Gregory is now free. I wonder if he will welcome the figure he finds on his doorstep this morning.

Books on Prescription

Upstairs in Nonfiction, beside the 'Health Information' shelving, is a section labelled 'BOP': Books on Prescription. These are books designed to encourage self-help. 'Reading Well' is a national scheme, and 'Reading Well Books on Prescription' are self-help books for managing common conditions including stress, depression, anxiety and dementia. The books are recommended by health experts and people with experience of the condition, and have been tried and tested and found to be useful.

The act of reading any book is apparently beneficial. A 2009 study by the University of Sussex unearthed the fact that reading silently to oneself reduces stress levels by up to 69 per cent – an astonishingly precise statistic. Reading slows down the heart rate and causes changes in the left temporal cortex, an area of the brain associated with language comprehension and a phenomenon known as 'embodied cognition'. This function allows neurons to trick the mind into thinking it's doing something that it is not.

The library recently surveyed its customers asking them to choose their favourite 'Mood Boosting' books. The top twenty were publicised, displayed on a table, and the list printed on bookmarks. They included *Jonathan Livingston Seagull*, Richard Bach, *Alice's Adventures in Wonderland* and *Through the Looking-glass*, Lewis Carroll, *The Necessary Aptitude*, Pam Ayres, *Diary of a Wimpy Kid*, Jeff Kinney, *The Unlikely Pilgrimage of Harold Fry*, Rachel Joyce, and *The Night Circus*, Erin Morgenstern.

Like pharmacists, I'm sure, librarians can't help but read something of the symptoms of their customers by the medicine they've been prescribed – or, in the case of the library, are self-administering. It doesn't take a degree in psychology to draw an inference from the young woman who has borrowed *Overcoming Anxiety* for the fourth time. More unsettling is a woman I have seen a number of times in the Nonfiction section. Painfully thin, she sits alone, reading a single book which is always squared neatly before her on the desk. The desk is always otherwise completely free of clutter. She reads without making contact with the table, her arms hanging loose by her sides. I don't know what she reads at her table, but the book she takes out again and again (six times at the last count) is *Cry of Pain*. It's a book subtitled 'understanding the suicidal mind'. I am always glad to see her at her table, alone and reading her single book.

Today provides another unsettling moment. I am in Children's. A timid, tall, young Mexican woman in an ankle-length black coat arrives at the desk with her sleeping child in a pushchair and her daughter (around three) holding tightly to her hand. Shyly the woman puts her four books for issue on the counter. I thank her. Silently she offers her card. The first three books I scan are large picture books. The final one is also masquerading as a picture book although the colours of the child on the cover are muted. As I issue it I see that the title is: *Is Daddy Coming Back in a Minute?* The authors are Elke and Alex Barber – I assume to be husband and wife. The subtitle is 'Explaining sudden death to children in words they can understand'. The Mexican woman takes the book from me and puts it into her hessian bag. Her face remains impassive as she pushes the pushchair away, her toddler trailing after her.

The image of the three of them stays with me. When I search for the book on the net I learn that the writers aren't husband and wife. Elke is actually Alex's mother. When Alex was three, his father died of a heart attack. The book was written as the result of conversations Elke had with her son. On her website she writes:

This, our first book, explains the concept of death in words very young children can understand. It is based on the conversations I had with my three-year-old son Alex, written in his own words. It gives gentle, yet honest answers to all those difficult questions that followed after his father died so suddenly. Sometimes being honest meant saying 'I don't know', and sometimes it meant going beyond what I might previously have thought of as 'acceptable'. To my toddler there was no difference between asking 'How does an aeroplane stay in the air?' and 'What happened to Daddy's body?' – he was simply looking for answers; he needed to understand. The worst thing had already happened; the worst thing I could lose now was my children's trust.

Lost and Found

An elderly woman arrives at the main desk and hands me a small black wallet.

'I found it on the London Road,' she tells me. 'There's a library card in it so I thought I'd bring it here.'

I thank her. She's not a member of the library and has taken the trouble to walk a mile out of her way to return the wallet. I radio Facilities. Facilities Steph retrieves the wallet and tells me she will report the find to the police in case the loser of the wallet phones up for it.

The trouble some people take to return lost property to their owners – especially wallets – is not uncommon.

A couple of weeks before I was at one of the branch libraries. It was the dead hour between 6 and 7 p.m. The clock hands were moving slowly towards closing time. The phone rang. I answered with the customary greeting.

'Hello?' I heard.

'Yes. Hello.'

'Hello?' It was a man's voice, pitched slightly loud – a north-eastern accent, soft Geordie. I heard a single car go past in the background, the high, swirling frequencies of the tyres on a wet road.

'Wait a mo',' the man said. 'I'm going back in.'

After a brief pause I heard a door opening, the sound of a radio playing pop music, a door closing.

'Can you hear me now?' the man asked. I replied that I could.

'So I've got this wallet,' he said.

'A wallet?'

'Yes. I'm in Northumberland. Near Hexham. I run a garage.'

'OK.' I pictured an Edward Hopper-like scene – three red old-fashioned petrol pumps, the soft orange glow of the lights. A tiny, lit hut. The human condition personified as a gas station.

'So there's a few credit cards in it and things and a few notes. And a library card from your library.'

'Ah.'

'So I just wondered if you'd have the number of the lady so I could call her and give her the wallet back.'

I explained that we can't give out personal numbers but if he'd give me his number I could call the woman and put her in touch. He did so.

I looked up the woman's account details from her card number and called the mobile phone number. A woman answered. Having explained the situation I asked her if she'd like the number of the garage man so she could retrieve her wallet.

'It's not my wallet,' the woman explained. 'It's my twin sister's.'

'Ah.'

'She's totally chaotic. We're not alike in any respect – except for our looks. For some reason she must have put my mobile down instead of hers.'

'You've got her number?'

'Of course. She's on some kind of wild goose chase after a man in Northumberland. It's not uncommon. She spent three

163

weeks in a commune last year. She said she was going to stay for the rest of her life but it didn't work out. Man trouble.'

Her sister told me she would pass on the information.

In contrast to the Good Samaritans, there are of course those who see other people's property as fair game. As often occurs, a customer comes to the main desk to report that his mobile has been stolen. He left it unattended, charging on a windowsill, and when he returned it was gone. Trev has warned him a number of times that it's inadvisable to leave valuables around but he prefers to trust (Japanese and Chinese students are the worst in this respect, routinely leaving shiny new Apple laptops or tablets on communal desks when they go out for lunch). Facilities are radioed. Trev arrives. The scene of the theft is pointed out to him. He smiles and looks towards the ceiling, inviting us, by implication, to do the same. What the thief has not counted on is that the area in which the phone was charging is covered by CCTV. Trev, rubbing his hands, returns to his lair to replay the footage.

This is what he sees: A thirty-something man sits reading the *Independent* newspaper. He's a well-dressed man in casuals and cycling shorts – nothing remarkable. He has just spent an hour on a PC in the IT Suite and seems to be killing time. As he looks around the room he spots the phone on the windowsill, charging, close to him. His eyes return to the paper. Now he's processing the odds – he's no longer reading. He looks again at the phone, this time more briefly. He doesn't want to attract attention to himself. A decision is made.

He stands, drops the *Independent* on the table and goes to a display rack beside the door, where he picks up a local free-sheet. He glances through it, looks around the room and then makes a beeline for the windowsill. He covers the phone with the paper on the pretext of looking out of the window and removes the charger from the socket. Pocketing both, unhurriedly, he leaves the library. Cut to the CCTV camera covering the door and the street outside. Here, the man is seen crossing the road and unlocking a cycle from a bike rack. He then cycles off, towards town.

The man has made two mistakes – not only being caught red-handed on CCTV but also using a library PC for an hour before he stole the phone. PCs are booked against a card. Customer accounts carry the residential details of the borrower. The man's address is furnished to the police, who come in to collect the footage. He is arrested the following day.

Late in the afternoon, supertramp Gareth Junior comes in to say goodbye and to tell me he is leaving tomorrow for Copenhagen.

I wish him a good journey. It has taken him many months but he has saved the fare. It's an evening flight but he is intending to walk to the airport.

'Thirty miles?' I tell him.

'Oh yes, thirty miles. Nothing. I'm leaving first thing.'

I wish him well. We shake hands. As I leave him, the picture of him trooping along thirty miles of dual carriageway worries me. I catch up with Gareth at the door and offer him a note.

'Get the train,' I say.

'No.'

'Please.'

Gareth takes the note and tucks it into his shirt pocket. He smiles, presses his palms together and inclines his head. 'Namaste,' he says. 'Namaste.'

And finally, something to warm the heart. Trev tells me that Brewer was in a few days ago. He's not been seen for a while but he came in because he'd found a mobile phone in the city centre and he didn't want to hand it in to the police because he thought it would get nicked by them.

Trev accepted it, charged it and, through phoning up the first couple of numbers, traced the owner – who was hugely relieved. Brewer was in the library when she arrived to collect her phone. Trev explained the circumstances of its return. She found Brewer in his usual place with his paper and thanked him. As a reward she then gave him enough for a night in a hostel.

Brewer was drunk for three days on the proceeds.

Spencer the Rover

Spencer is a tall, gentle, genial Irish busker. He arrives with
Brewer, Wolf and the others each morning and takes refuge
beside his usual pillar, where he remains for much of the
morning, reading an eclectic collection of cutting-edge
economic treatises or comic books. The street people rarely
use the seats in the centre of the room, instead choosing those
places where there's something solid at their back. Survival
conditioning runs deep. Most afternoons Spencer wanders to
the desk with a CD and his mandolin case to ask to use the
'Listening Post'. The listening post is, as its name suggests, a
CD machine fixed to the wall where customers can audition
audio through headphones before they rent it – rather like the
booths in the record shops of the 1950s and 1960s. Spencer,
not having a formal home to speak of, uses it as his personal
entertainment system. I ask him about the CD he's asked to
hear. It's the most recent one by Ed Sheeran.

'I promised him I'd check it out,' Spencer says, smiling.

'Ed Sheeran?'

'Yes.'

'You know him?'

'He played here last week and I was out busking. He gave me
a tenner.'

Sometimes your faith is temporarily restored in humanity.

I unlock the listening post, insert the CD and leave Spencer standing happily (he never sits at the listening post) listening to Ed Sheeran's latest offering.

Occasionally I see Spencer around the city. He stands in doorways playing his plaintive and haunting folk tunes on his mandolin. He sings well. He's fascinated by the history of folk and occasionally hitches up to London to Cecil Sharp House, where he spends the day in the folk music library to find new material. He's chosen his life. He gives little away about his history, but he is content and well-adjusted to his off-the-grid life. Only once did he mention working in an office, but it seems the life didn't suit him. He keeps himself apart from the other street sleepers and is currently borrowing a sofa from somebody he knows on the north edge of the city. He busks and never begs, but he knows where he can find the occasional sofa for the night or which restaurant is doing the soup run in the winter.

A week or so later I am walking through a local park at the beginning of the day. A travelling fair has taken over the space. Robbed of the cover of night, the naked light bulbs unilluminated, it looks like a garish crime scene. There's no sign of movement from any of the caravans. Curtains are drawn across steamed-up windows. Then Spencer emerges with his bedroll and mandolin case. He might have come out of a caravan or, indeed, have slept beneath one of them or perhaps under the trees. Like psychiatrists, when librarians encounter their clients outside the library they usually do not acknowledge them. Spencer walks on.

I mention him to a couple of neighbours a week or so later. They know him and I learn that one night he had his mandolin stolen. The incensed customers of the pub outside which he often performed had a whip round and bought him a new one.

Spencer the Rover seems an appropriate theme tune to his existence:

> A valiant a man as ever left home,
> and he had been much reduced
> which caused great confusion,
> and that was the reason he started to roam.

WINTER

WINTER

Torah

An elderly, small, Jewish man, beady-eyed, approaches the counter, wheezing hard. He is wearing no coat but has a sensible V-neck jumper on. His hair is neatly cut; indeed, 'neat' is perhaps the best way to describe this compact individual. He is carrying a large, scarlet-boxed copy of the Torah.

'Hello,' he says cheerily.

'Hello.'

'Do you have the facilities for photocopying?'

'Yes, we do.'

Immediately he holds up the first finger of his right hand in a cautionary 'don't be so hasty' gesture. 'But can you increase the size of the print?'

I explain that it is possible but it's not very straightforward – years of training in the vagaries of the machine are required but I suggest we could put our heads together and have a bash. He thanks me, puts his Torah on the counter, slides it from the slipcase and looks at the words, reading them silently to himself.

'English,' he begins, looking up from the text. 'When you read English out loud, it's like you can hear the pages speaking to you. Do you understand what I'm saying?' I say that I do.

'This here.' He points to a page of symbols. 'I can read this fluently. It's like music.' He reads for a while – this time out loud

173

– it's hypnotic. 'I can read it but I can't understand it.' He reads out a little more. 'Music. Can you make this larger?' He taps the page gently.

'I'll try.'

Together, we puzzle the intricacies of the photocopier. I copy three sheets.

'This is for my grandson. It's his bar mitzvah. I'm listening to check his pronunciation.'

He reads a little more, then breaks off and turns to me: 'How old do you think I am?' he asks me.

Always a tricky question to answer. He looks to be in his late eighties. I deduct about fifteen years for safety's sake: 'Seventy-five?'

'I'm eighty-nine!' He laughs gleefully.

'No!'

'Yes. I am. Eighty-nine!'

This leads him into a brief historical diversion into the Jewish diaspora, in the course of which he tells me he is an Ashkenazi Jew. 'Do you know anything about the Ashkenazi?'

I admit that when it comes to Judaism there's a large gap in my knowledge. He runs through a few salient points in the history. I ask him about his profession.

'I was a ladies' pattern cutter,' he says proudly and he seems to grow in height a couple of inches. 'I can look at any lady and immediately know her size.'

'Did you work locally?'

'London. Then I moved here when I married. I've worked in Johannesburg, Tel Aviv, New York. All over.'

The copying is done.

'I've had a good life,' he says. He seems content; at peace. 'In conclusion, could I ask you to do me a small favour?'

'Of course.'

'My braces.' He turns his back to me, turning his head to face me over his right shoulder. 'They've come off. Could you help me?'

'Of course.'

It's an intimate moment. I reach up inside the back of the old man's blue V-neck woollen jumper and locate the end of his braces. His back is warm. He smells of talcum powder.

'Just a single end?' I ask.

'Yes. Just one.'

I pull it down, feeling it stretch against the gentle resistance of the elastic and attach the brass clasp to the waistband of his trousers.

'Ah, that's better.' He turns to face me and offers his hand to be shaken. 'Thank you for your help.'

We shake hands.

'Thanks for the history lesson.'

'My pleasure.'

Smiling, he walks off with his enlarged print copies.

For a while I think of my father and wonder what he's doing today and regret we live so far away.

An Extra Roast Potato

A man in orange trousers, fair hair, blue puffa jacket, clutching a litre bottle of water (half drunk), waves me ahead of him to get into the lift. The doors slide shut.

'I worked in an office for thirty years,' he says. 'Up and down the stairs fifty times a day. I reckon I've earned the lift.'

I agree with him.

'I lived in Switzerland. On a mountain,' he volunteers as the lift sails up towards Nonfiction. 'Wife and two kids. The oldies used to climb up the mountains and take the cable car down. Going down was bad for the knees, they said. I learned from that.'

He leaves the lift, heads for the main room, but then pauses, turns and scurries back to say something else. Retrieving his glasses from his man bag, he says, 'Remembered my specs! Luxury. Being able to see. Like getting an extra roast potato.'

Nonfiction is quiet and reluctantly, having alphabetically ordered the books on the returns trolley, I wheel it from behind the service point and begin shelving. I'm glad to see that somebody else has borrowed Manguel's *Library at Night* and slip it into its place among the other Dewey 020 books (020 is Library and Information Sciences). Whatever the benefits of the internet for information gathering it will rarely provide the serendipity of a library shelf. In Nonfiction, a book's neighbours can be as enticing as the book you've just read. Two books along the row I spot one I haven't seen before: *Hitler's Private Library: The Books that Shaped His Life* by Timothy W. Ryback. I slot it onto the trolley in the gap left by Manguel's book and, when the shelving is done, begin to look through it. Ryback tells us that the man better remembered for burning books, by the time he died at the age of fifty-six, owned an estimated 16,000 volumes and ranked *Don Quixote* along with *Robinson Crusoe*, *Uncle Tom's Cabin* and *Gulliver's Travels* among the great works of world literature.[15]

Another writer, William Shirer, notes propaganda minister Goebbels' list of authors recommended for burning. They included Heinrich Mann, Stefan Zweig, Freud, Zola, Proust, Gide, Helen Keller and H. G. Wells. The act of incinerating these authors' works allowed 'the soul of the German people again to express itself. These flames not only illuminate the final end of an old era; they also light up the new.'[16]

What's interesting, beyond what Hitler chose to put on his shelves, is what happened to the books after his death. According to Ryback, the entire Reich Chancellery library – an estimated 10,000 volumes – was secured by a Soviet 'trophy brigade' and shipped to Moscow and never seen again. 'The only significant portions of Hitler library's [*sic*] to survive intact were the three thousand books discovered in the Berchtesgaden salt mine, twelve hundred of which made it into the Library of Congress.' Thousands more apparently lie on the bookshelves of veterans across the United States (and presumably the rest of the world) but occasionally random volumes find their way to the public: 'Several years ago, a copy of Peter Maag's *Realm of God and the Contemporary World*, published in 1915, with "A. Hitler" scrawled on the inside cover, was discovered in the fifty cent bin of a local library sale in upstate New York.'[17]

The value of these books raises an interesting moral question. Albert Aronson was part of the American delegation sent to Berlin to negotiate the joint occupation of the city. His Soviet hosts took him on a tour of Hitler's private quarters and, as a courtesy, let him take an unclaimed pile of eighty books. Following Aronson's death, his nephew donated the books to Brown University. In the early 1990s Daniel Traister, head of the rare book collection at the University of Pennsylvania, was given several of Hitler's books. They were accompanied by a note which read: 'Dan, you wouldn't believe how much money people want to offer me for these things. So far, I haven't met one whom I want to have them. Here: destroy them or keep them as you wish.'[18]

Manguel tells a remarkable story Vladimir Nabokov relates in one of his letters, which also comes from the period of German retreat. In May 1945, when Russian troops were entering Prague, the librarian Elena Sikorskaja, Nabokov's sister,

> realized that the German officers now attempting to retreat had not returned several of the books they had borrowed from the library she worked in. She and a colleague decided to reclaim the truant volumes, and set out on a rescue mission through the streets down which the Russian trucks were victoriously bundling. 'We reached the house of a German pilot who returned the books quite calmly,' she wrote to her brother a few months later.[19]

Hitler's library haunts me for the rest of the day but I'm diverted by an hour in Children's, where a worried-faced young girl arrives at the desk and proffers a picture book entitled *Do You Want to Be My Friend?*

'It's ripped,' she says. 'I don't really like ripped books.'

'Neither do I. Shall we mend it?'

'Yes.'

I hunt for the sticky tape in the drawer. She holds the page flat and we repair the book. It seems to meet her approval as she returns with it to her spot on the carpet.

Meanwhile, a toddler is kneeling on one of the PC seats and has been for ten minutes. She has something pressed to her ear and is listening intently. I assume she's listening to YouTube on headphones. On closer inspection I see that she is not logged into the PC and has the computer mouse to her ear. Who knows what intergalactic frequency she is tuned in to, but she is content and unmoving.

As the hour in Children's is about to end a woman comes up to the counter, stands quite close and whispers that there's something she needs to tell me.

'I don't want to frighten the other mothers,' she says, and leaves the statement hanging there.

'Frighten them how?'

'A man came out of the toilets and looked very sheepish. I think he was using the cubicle for drugs.'

'How could you tell?'

'As I said, he looked very sheepish.'

'Sheepish?'

'Yes. And he had a white tracksuit on. He looked like a druggie.'

'OK, I'll tell Security.'

I can already picture Trev's response to the profile – sheepish, white tracksuit, looks like a druggy: the description could be applied to a significant number of the customers.

'It's not very good, in the children's library, to have drug users nipping in and out,' the woman goes on.

'But why do you assume he's using drugs?'

'I just know. You can tell.'

I have no choice but to explain to her that the toilets are for general use and unless the man is caught in the act, injecting heroin into one of his few remaining functioning veins or perhaps his eyeball, there's very little we can do. I assure her that Facilities keep a close eye on known and suspected drug users and police them closely. The woman, unconvinced, leaves.

I follow her up the slope into the main library and see Trev chewing the fat with one of the regulars. He breaks off.

'All right, young man?'

'Customer is worried that somebody is shooting up in Children's.'

'Yeah? What did he look like?'

'Thin. White tracksuit.'

'Oh, him. Yeah, I've just seen him. We know him. Pain in the whatsit, but not a user.'

Trev, apologising to the regular, beckons for me to follow him into the Large Print section, where the white track-suited man is using a PC. 'That's him.'

Now I recognise the man. He's a new regular; a street sleeper who arrives with his girlfriend – a rare, female street sleeper. She is large – perhaps twenty stone, the same height but approximately twice the width of the man – and the contents of their belongings are usually strewn around the Young People's area while they lie snuggled together on the sofas and sleep for as long as they can before Trev or another of the team spots them and turfs them out. The smell of the pair of them is indescribably bad and has been worsening over the last weeks.

'Yeah, we know him,' Trev tells me. 'Charles. That's his name.'

No surprise there, Trev knows everybody.

'Three kids with three different women.' He looks at me to test my reaction. I try to remain neutral. 'Know what?'

'What?'

'She's pregnant.'

I look across at the large woman. She knows she's being discussed. She looks back towards us – challenging us.

'Move them to the top of the housing register, won't it?' Trev smiles, pats me on the shoulder and returns to the man he was talking to.

Paranoia

In the morning the gap between the pizza restaurant and the hotel allows the winter sun onto the piazza. The long cube of white widens as the morning goes on. Today, there's a furry ball, dead centre of the cube, throwing a long shadow. On closer inspection it's a pigeon, chest puffed out, warming itself and catching an early sleep.

The soundtrack to the morning's Van Box processing is pitched way too loud for the staff fighting hangovers. It's the Yeah Yeah Yeahs – ungentle, grungy New York music. I pad wearily towards the most junior member of staff and ask why he considered the music appropriate for this ungodly hour of the day. He shrugs, smiles and tells me the choice was not his, but that of one of our senior female colleagues, early/mid-sixties, happily shelving the returns, skipping along as she does so. The cacophony continues until a manager arrives for the briefing and turns the CD player off. It feels like school – I expect him to ask for the culprit to raise his or her hand.

Storm clouds are gathering both literally and metaphorically. This morning, as I walked the short distance to the library, I looked up to see a black cloud with a ruler-straight bottom edge sitting on a white slab of sky. The talk here is of impending cuts. The rumours were accurate. Like at all councils, the next round will be savage – there's no more flesh on the bones. Libraries will close, or open with shortened hours, or operate without staff. Pilots are being run in two of the community libraries in which users can get in with special cards and, observed by CCTV, use the library without humans in attendance.

Library visits have fallen over the past year by some 10 million but it remains the most popular leisure activity in the country. With the apparent success of Suffolk and York as library mutuals (a social enterprise model in which the staff and the public share mutual ownership), more authorities are thinking the same way. There are already thirty or so trusts running library services in the UK.

The organisation currently identified in the news as 'the "so-called" Islamic State' has perpetrated another atrocity. This is the week in which 130 unarmed people are shot dead in Paris. It seems likely that the UK will be targeted and the morning's staff briefing is sober and formal. We are advised to be vigilant; to watch bags and immediately to report anything suspicious to the managers or Facilities.

At a little before 11 a.m. an announcement is made that, should they wish to, the public can join the minute's silence in support of the people of Paris. The minute is generally observed although there are mutterings that we showed no such solidarity with the people of Beirut or Palestine when similar atrocities were perpetrated there.

At midday I go upstairs to Nonfiction, taking the staff lift rather than the public stairs. I enter the room along a short corridor that leads from the lift to the main floor. A security-coded door prevents public access to the staff area. The corridor is used occasionally for young lovers to meet, sit on the carpet and snog instead of getting on with the schoolwork they're presumably supposed to be doing. There are two alcoves in this corridor, around four feet square. Today, in the alcove closest to the staff door, are two men. Both are kneeling on the carpet, facing the wall. One is perhaps African, the other Middle Eastern – early/mid-thirties. On the floor between them is an exercise book. I can see that street names have been listed neatly on the pages. One of the men is talking into a mobile phone, the other is leafing through the book. Also on the floor is a Bible, which is open. The men don't look up as I pass them. I stop and turn and look back towards them and I think of Paris.

In a quiet corner I radio Facilities – telling them my location and that I need their assistance. Trev and Steph interrupt their tea-break and arrive smartly. I lead them to a vantage point to observe the men. Trev agrees that I have reasonable grounds for suspicion. They discuss what to do. Steph is deputed to ask the men if they'd like to take their work to an open table while Trev monitors from a distance. She will explain that the corridor is a fire route and cannot be blocked. We watch her approach and then stand over them. One and then the other man look up at her. As planned she suggests to them that they use one of the large communal tables in the centre of the room. The men gather their belongings. Instead of moving to the table they take the staircases to the exit and leave the building.

'What do you think?' Trev asks Steph.

'Not sure.'

'Shall we bell them? Your call.'

The discussion continues about whether the police should be alerted. A manager is called. The CCTV is reviewed. The Bible is the factor that sways it – an unlikely prop for a member of the 'so-called' Islamic State. As the discussion continues on the ground floor one of the men comes back in – the Middle

Eastern man. Trev identifies him to the manager who falls into step with him and they move out of earshot.

Later, the manager seeks me out. He wants to let me know the outcome of the conversation he had. The man, it seems, is doing 'The Knowledge'. His friend was helping him to learn the street names. The Bible belonged to his friend, an Evangelist on his way to a prayer meeting.

For the following couple of weeks, levels of paranoia continue to remain high. At another library I'm watching a woman trying to herd a child into Children's when a man approaches the desk. He wears shoulder-length, grey, tangled hair. He is thin, in denim head to foot – a refugee from the 1960s.

'Can you help me?' he asks. His voice carries a trace of transatlantic drawl. I tell him I'll do what I can.

'I can't get into Google.' He laughs – a private joke with himself. 'Again.'

I accompany him to the PC he's booked and attempt to open Google. It refuses to launch.

'CIA,' he says.

'CIA?'

He laughs again – perhaps trying to head off my incredulity. He seems rational enough.

'They're keeping an eye on me. Monitoring my movements.'

'OK . . .'

'Yeah, well . . .' He offers no more – the 'well' is an acknowledgement that he knows, from the outside, the notion is ludicrous, and he does not expect me to believe it.

'Let's try another PC.'

I log the man into the next PC. A woman has been using it for an hour and has reported no issues with it – there are none of the usual cries of complaint from the assembled computer users that the internet has gone down. Using his account log in, the PC will not load Google nor will it load any other search engine. By now a queue has formed at the counter. I apologise to the man and tell him that I have to deal with it but, if he has no luck, I will return and help him when I can.

By the time the customers have been cleared, the man has left the PC and is passing the desk. I apologise that I didn't have time to return to him. He tells me, 'It's no big deal.' I wait.

This is the story he tells. I offer the facts as he related them:

He was born in a small south coast town in the mid-1940s. His father had a light aircraft and taught him to fly. By sixteen he was a competent pilot. It was easier then to get a licence. He was looking for a thrill. The Vietnam War was at its height. He heard that the Americans were recruiting pilots so he went to the United States and joined the Navy as a flyer. He was shipped to Vietnam, where he flew Hunters, F18s and other planes. He acknowledged how odd it now sounds but assured me that his experience was not uncommon. A number of US Air Force and Navy pilots came from overseas – guns for hire. But as his political understanding grew, he became disillusioned. One day he walked away from the base, went back to his apartment and refused to come out. They sent two men for him in a jeep. He returned. After that, things become hazy. He remembers being shipped out on a US aircraft carrier and being taken down into a room, where he was questioned. He remembers two other men were in the room with him, getting the same treatment at the same time from two other men. It was dark: grey, dull metal walls. 'They mess with your mind,' he said. 'It's noise – images. They tried to wipe my mind.' A few days later, one of the other men was found dead in his bunk. Somehow – he doesn't quite know how – he got away, defected. He flew MIGs for the Soviets for a while, and then went elsewhere, making a living as a pilot (crop spraying, small commercial flights) into his early thirties when he returned to the UK.

He's a tree surgeon now. He doesn't have a computer at home because he knows they're still watching him. He has a network of contacts and he knows who the bad guys are. There are a lot of them around watching him, watching us.

Cycle Lane

A charabanc of library managers from around the country is visiting to see how we do things. As libraries continue to be hacked away, cash-strapped authorities are sharing ideas. What the visitors don't expect to see (although the staff here barely look up from their service points) is an elderly gentleman on a racing cycle tearing into the library entrance at breakneck speed and performing two circuits of the shop.

One of the managers breaks from the tour group, sprints across the floor and demands my radio. I don't have one. He rushes to another desk and grabs one to call Trev. Trev appears rapidly (ish) from his den, tailed a few steps behind by another of the Facilities staff – Robin to his Batman.

I've not been in for a week and have missed the earlier cyclist episodes so, intrigued, I follow Trev, the manager, and his helper out of the main doors where a man – lean, late sixties, long flowing grey hair (bald on top) in Lycra leggings and what look like grey hot pants – is circling the piazza at some speed. He is impervious to the calls from the door of the library, instead seems to be revelling in teasing them. Each circuit brings him closer to the door, but the speed he's travelling would make it impossible to stop him without sustaining major injury. The police have been called but will not arrive in time because now the cyclist leaves the piazza and heads off up the narrow street and towards the north of the town, where he is lost to view.

More details are related after the incident. The cyclist has now been seen four times inside the library. He appears usually late morning, does a couple of circuits of the shop and then speeds out again. Earlier, somebody put their arm out to try and unseat him but he drove past. He'll be back and Trev and Robin will get him.

Violent and challenging customers are common to libraries the world over. America, inevitably, has its own extreme versions. Steve Albrecht was a cop with the San Diego police and now runs a programme called 'the difficult patron' for a number of American libraries. In *Psychology Today*, he wrote about his experiences:

At my first training sessions, I began to hear tales of staff having to deal with obnoxious, entitled, and dangerous patrons. Libraries attract the poor and the bewildered, the opportunistic crook and the sneak thief, gang members, abandoned or runaway kids, people who can't control their Axis II disorders or sobriety, and the sexual predator who prefers children, or at least the pornography enthusiast who doesn't have his own computer or access to the Internet . . . Younger female staff members told me how they would get stalked by library patrons because they wore nametags with their first and last names and job titles on them. The perpetrators would use the branch computers to find out personal information about them.[20]

He argues that free use of the internet is at the root of the problems. Asking his training groups to identify the one thing that could make their facility a better, safer place to work, getting rid of the internet was always at the top of the list.

Staffers tell me the story is the same every morning before they open: a long line of homeless people or other aggressive patrons push and shove their way over to the Internet computers, often at a dead run. They spend hours on these machines, and intimidate other patrons or even staff members who try to move them along so other people can have a turn.

As I begin to walk back to the main desk, Trev beckons me towards the security booth. 'Got a minute?'

I haven't, but I follow Trev in. The room is small, around eight feet square. The left side is dominated by a large shelf and the ding-dong machine (tannoy announcements). To the left of it is the safe. The right wall is where Facilities have pasted up printed images of suspected felons with a brief précis of the crime. The wall facing the door is alight with CCTV screens. The bottom, central screen, is frozen on pause.

'Look at this,' Trev says and prompts the screen into action. 'This was last Thursday night.' We watch the action unfold: The entrance doors viewed from above, pooled in a yellow milky light. They slide open. A man – one of the street regulars – appears, Trev behind him, behind Trev a female manager. The man head-butts the pillar which houses the security bleeps, turns towards Trev. Trev ushers him out. He's moving out of shot as he head-butts Trev. The drama is over.

'Nice way to end the day,' Trev reflects.

The Season to Be Chilly

Pre-briefing, conversation revolves around the relatively recent festivities and the imminent exodus of a number of the long-serving staff. Most report having had a 'quiet Christmas'. Over the past thirty or forty years I've yet to talk to anyone who bucked the trend and had a boisterous time.

Sons of Anarchy Alan is in first thing. He's in negotiation with a member of staff at the main desk because he's trying to take out three boxed sets of *SOA* but still has three at home that are long overdue and are blocking any more borrowing until they are returned. He's sanguine and makes to leave, slightly wearily. Today, he's wearing a Chelsea FC bobble hat and a Chelsea backpack. I ask him about the progress of his tattoos.

'Soon,' he says, brightening a little. He shakes my hand.

'It's the season,' Facilities Bob announces as he comes across the floor and stands at my shoulder. Bob's older than the others in the team and had another life in education before joining the squad. Facilities have seen it all, but Bob has also seen it from another angle. He's eyeing two of the regular troublemakers who are sitting in the comfy seats by the magazines. Both are awake, sober and behaving.

'Couple of months ago,' he begins, 'one of the regulars went downstairs to the toilet. The door was locked so he pissed up against it. Couldn't believe it when I told him it was unacceptable. Unbelievable. I took him by the collar and chucked him out.'

When Facilities stand behind you at the service points, chances are they're eyeing somebody up. I ask who the current suspect is. Facilities Bob explains that the culprit is gone but he's waiting for him to return. He's another book thief – but he knows the system. His modus operandi is to take out a book and then to return with it, carrying it visibly under his arm. He then goes to the shelves, takes down another book, rips out the security tag and then puts that book alongside the other as he leaves the library. Neither book triggers the alarm and were he ever to be challenged he could proffer the legitimately issued book as evidence to support his innocence. Facilities Bob scouts the floor around the shelving for a tell-tale tag, but can't see one.

'Saw him at Oxfam last week,' Bob tells me. 'I told the woman at the counter that he was in nicking books. He legged it, but I saw him pacing up and down the pavement outside. I don't know why he does it. He's not poor.'

Bob turns his attention to a middle-aged, casually dressed man at one of the PCs. He saw him talking to me at the main desk earlier in the day and asks if he was after some free extra time on the computer. I tell him that he wanted to extend his booking but he was happy to pay. The man is Liverpudlian. He's polite and seems reasonable enough. As Bob and I talk, the Liverpudlian approaches the counter and asks me to keep an eye on his computer while he goes to retrieve a sandwich from his car. When he's out of earshot Bob tells me that the man is not quite what he appears.

'No?'

'Lives in his motor.'

'What?'

'He's been living in his car for a month. He comes in here

192

each day to use the PCs and to wash, and each night, he drives away to sleep in it somewhere.'

'How do you know?'

'He told me. He's come south looking for a job. Hard times.'

Bob wants to share one more story about book thieves: 'Couple of years back, the manager here got a call from the police. They didn't say what it was about but they wanted to come and pick her up and accompany them somewhere. Anyway, they came and picked her up. Didn't tell her anything. Drove her to the edge of town. Got out of the car. Big Victorian block. Went down the steps to the basement. She followed them in. All the rooms were full of books. Thousands of them, floor-to-ceiling. All nicked from the libraries here. It took three vanloads to get them back. Old boy lived there. He wasn't poor. Why would he do it?'

A number of surveys have been done on the books most regularly stolen from libraries. *The Guinness Book of Records* regularly heads the table followed usually by the Bible, then books designed to help for exam preparation (one US blogger suggests law-enforcement officer training manuals are among the most commonly stolen exam prep books), 'racy' books and manuals – *Kama Sutra*, art books with nudes in them and erotica – art books generally (high value) and, more predictably, reference works.

The most notorious and prodigious book thief of recent years is Marino Massimo De Caro, former director of the Baroque-era Girolamini Library in Naples. When he was appointed in 2011 the library was in chaos and had been closed for a few years despite having a stock of priceless, centuries-old editions by the likes of Aristotle, Descartes, Galileo and Machiavelli. Things didn't improve. Hearing rumours that the library remained in trouble after De Caro's appointment, Tomaso Montanari (modern art history professor, writer and blogger) visited there in the spring of 2012. He was shocked by what he found: 'There was a dog roaming around the library with a bone in its mouth! There were books spread around everywhere – on the floor, on the stairs, on tables. There was garbage – soda cans and papers – on the floor. It was total confusion, a situation of major decay.'[21] During his visit a member of staff suggested that the director was stealing from the library. Montanari wrote an article for the *Il Fatto Quotidiano* newspaper in which he stated that having De Caro as librarian was like 'having an arsonist in charge of a forest'. The library was closed by the public prosecutor and 1,000 rare books were found at De Caro's home in Verona. Investigations revealed he'd also stolen from other libraries in Italy, including Montecassino, the Naples Municipal Library, the Ministry of Agriculture Library, a seminary in Padua and the Ximines Observatory Library in Florence. He was suspected of being responsible for the theft of 4,000 rare books and was given a seven-year prison sentence. But he didn't operate alone. Thirteen others were also charged, including a priest.

The temptation for people like De Caro and his gang grows as the value of books increases. *The Bay Psalm Book*, the first book printed in English in North America, became the most expensive ever bought at auction when it sold for $14,165,000 in 2013. Sotheby's confirmed that it was purchased by American financier and philanthropist David Rubenstein 'who planned to loan it to libraries across the country'.

Unfortunately, this library has no copy of *The Bay Psalm Book* among its stock of rare books. There are, however, around 40,000 of them in an air-conditioned, fire-retardant vault on the Nonfiction floor. The stock was protected and curated by an experienced and committed librarian who worked hard to promote the extraordinary collection. She was among those who recently left the service, with her responsibilities subsumed into another post. The hope is that the new custodian cares as much for the stock and protects it fiercely from the De Caros of the world – and perhaps the local authorities when they begin to cast around more widely for ways to raise money.

The stock in the rare books room can be viewed under supervision. Today, there are two people in the glass-walled area reading quietly. But, at ten past four in the afternoon, the library is generally quiet. Silence is contagious. There are fifteen people ranged around the comfy chairs in Nonfiction reading books or newspapers, several more studying on the wide tables. There's an almost palpable sense of calm and within that calm I can feel my heartbeat actually slowing. As it does, I become aware of my breathing. As my mind quietens it offers up the image of a row of electrical cars tethered to their charging posts – the electricity flowing into them.

It doesn't last. A young man limps to the counter. The right leg of his denim jeans is ripped and blood-marked. He is wincing with pain. He tells me he has forgotten his library card but needs to use a computer so can I furnish him with his account number? For a few moments I resist asking why he is wincing and holding his leg but eventually succumb.

'Fell down a manhole,' he says. 'Up to here.' He draws a line across his upper chest with the ledge of his hand.

'How did you get out?'

'Somebody pulled me out. A woman. I'm emailing the council.'

'Don't blame you,' I say.

'Can I book some time on a PC?'

'Of course.'

Hunky Dory

The tenth of January 2016 and the nation wakes to the news that David Bowie has died after the inevitable 'long battle' with cancer – a battle nobody wins or, at least, when they do it's not reported. *Breakfast Time* wheeled out the usual talking heads. A particularly memorable quote from guitarist Mick Ronson's daughter, who was introduced as knowing Bowie and having worked with him. She immediately put the interviewer straight, explaining that she had done neither but was, nevertheless, extremely sad.

I stop to buy the daily cappuccino on the way in. The small, wooden-floored coffee shop is bereft of other customers. This city rises late. A friend once observed it's where the young go to retire. The new Bowie album is being played. I talk to the barista and he says that we all felt we knew Bowie. That's why there's an outpouring of grief. We knew him and somehow we feel we could have saved him. Inevitably, Bowie's greatest hits are being piped through the library as the morning's Van Boxes are attended to. Bowie was a great autodidact. One of the pundits reported that during a long trip across Russia he took a crate of books with him to read on the train. In this he shared a habit with Rabelais, who carried his 'portable library', a chest full of books, with him for the twenty years he spent wandering around Europe.

The staff and customers are subdued today. Some are nursing seasonal hangovers, which is perhaps why the xylophone hammer has gone missing in Children's, diminishing the noise emanating from that end of the building. It's a day of the regulars calling in. After a long absence Joseph is back but his daughter is not with him. He seems lost, makes for Children's then, seeming to remember, turns back, collects a copy of the *Telegraph* from the rack and takes it to one of the sofas. The Travelling Man is also in. He brings a Val McDermid to the counter and asks me to check if he's had it before. He has, in 2012. He holds his palm to his chest, which is rattling noisily.

'Need a new pair of lungs,' he says, trying to catch his breath, and returns to Crime in search of another book.

A toddler approaches the desk from the rear, smiles briefly, and then projectile vomits. It hits the floor and the wave stops just short of the rear of my right boot. Facilities are called and the ever-patient cleaner arrives with her mop and bucket, surveys the extent of the spillage and announces she is going for her heavy-duty apparatus. The other staff member in there says that yesterday afternoon they were playing 'Is it vomit or is it a kebab?' – a seasonal game in which the participants stand at the centre of the carpet in Children's and try to identify whatever has been deposited on it. Meanwhile, a young, ashen-faced Chinese woman has lost her handbag. It's expensive. It has a gold chain. Facilities are radioed and Trev reports that the bag has been handed in. He delivers it to the girl and she hugs him – the highlight of his day.

Security is still high on the agenda. A man in cycling Lycra asks if we have 'a policy on left bags'. I ask him to elucidate. He reports that a few minutes ago a young girl asked an elderly man to keep an eye on her suitcase in the IT Suite while she went out of the library to collect something. Cycling Man apologises for his suspicions but he says he remembers 1980. I assure him that he should report any suspicions. Facilities are alerted. CCTV is viewed. The elderly man who was looking after the woman's bag is informed that this kind of public spiritedness is, for the time being, unacceptable.

Spencer takes his place at the desk and hands over the CD he wants to listen to at the listening post. I take it from him: *Hunky Dory*, David Bowie. What else?

Waiting for Ted

An air of gloom, perhaps resignation, hangs over the library as the Van Boxes are processed. Yesterday the van broke down so the delivery today is twice the normal load and the green boxes are stacked high.

But redundancy packages have been now been calculated and offered in an attempt to cull the numbers of staff. Savings of around 30 per cent have to be made in the library's budget. The philosophy is to keep as many libraries open as possible with reduced staff numbers. Presumably the hope is that eventually there will be a sea change in attitude and local authority budgets increased, enabling these dormant institutions to spring back to life. The old-timers have seen this before, but not to this extent. The battle that was fought and won in the nineteenth century for a universal free service has broken out again and this time is being lost. Councils see libraries as a soft target, many of them conveniently forgetting they have a statutory responsibility to provide them.

Publisher-turned-philanthropist William Sieghart has been given a CBE in the New Year's Honours list for 'services to public libraries'. Sieghart chaired the independent review of libraries and in December 2014 produced a report on their future, which warned against the trend of volunteer-led libraries.

While Sieghart's work has been officially recognised, his actual report seems to have been all but forgotten. Over a hundred libraries closed last year.

In this authority the proposals are that some libraries will be single-staffed, two will be closed, and the number of staff in the main libraries reduced. Statutory council redundancy packages are derisory in comparison with the commercial world: four-figure sums for many of the longstanding staff. A senior woman bemoans the fact that she has been working in the service since 1992. She has been offered a redundancy payment of £9,000 and her annual pension will be £4,000. The word is that all staff members will have to reapply for their jobs, but the new jobs on offer all include at least one weekend day's working a week, many of them two. Morale is low and even the aggressive tones of Grace Jones emanating from the CD player don't lighten the mood before the morning's staff briefing.

The main item on the agenda is the recurring toilet blockages. The problem has flared up again. Children's suffered a nasty outpouring just before Christmas. The unblockers were called and, grim-faced, applied their machinery to the system. For a while it was cleared, but the problem is not solved so another flushing will be necessary until the experts can get to the root of the problem.

Today, in the community section, two men are sitting and talking intently. Between them, on the low table, is a large packet of crisps they have consumed. Spilling from the mouth of the crisp packet is orange peel. The peel perfumes the air. One of the men is bald headed, mid-thirties, glasses, a fully zipped anorak. The other is older, unshaven, also wearing glasses, a thick gold chain around his neck and a donkey jacket, overweight, slumped slightly forward in the comfy chair. A third man at the table is large and powerfully built. He's asleep with a smile on his face and looks like a circus strongman resting before tackling the next lift. I should wake him, but I haven't the heart. He's sleeping rough and the rain has been incessant for the past two weeks. He's welcome to the warmth and comfort for a few hours.

The two men at the table are discussing the government's new initiative to reduce the number of alcohol units consumed each day. They share the view that the suggested limit wouldn't even whet their whistles and the weekly limit is often reached in a single session. If anything, they view it as a target. Their lack of funds, however, is preventing them from going to 'The Spoons' (the local Wetherspoon's pub, reputed to have the cheapest beer in the city). They are waiting for Ted, who is late but whom they expect will stand them a few drinks. These are the functioning alcoholics who need their daily intake but still operate well enough to take manual work where they can find it.

After discussing their prodigious alcohol intake during the festival season, Greg is explaining his recent employment history. 'Well, I worked on the refuse and on the sweep. They had four companies, kept losing contracts, and each time I was taken on by the new one until I got fired. The first one was best. When you'd done a day on the wagon and came back in they offered you overtime so you turned round and went straight back out again.'

'Every day?'

'Yeah. Nearly every day.'

'And they paid you by the month?'

'Week. Good money.'

'How much?'

'Three hundred a week. Thereabouts.'

'Why were you sacked?'

'Late . . . few days got in late. Bad time. They gave me three warnings but then . . . You?'

'Went for a job in a charity shop just before Christmas.'

'Volunteer?'

'You're f***ing joking! Anyway, they asked for my boot size.'

'Why?'

'Dunno. And they said I needed a hi-vis jacket.'

'Why?'

'Dunno. They took my size.'

'Did you get it?'

'The jacket?'

'The job.'

'Dunno.'

'Heard from Ted?'

Mobile phone is checked. 'No.'

'New Year's Eve I went to the Spoons. Got there just after eleven in the morning. Left at two the following day.'

'Yeah?'

'Yeah.'

'Was Ted there?'

'I think so. Can't remember. No, I think his son was there.'

'Didn't do much New Year's.'

'Go out?'

'Oh yeah, went out but didn't do much.'

The conversation stalls. Greg reaches into the pocket of his donkey jacket and takes out another mandarin orange and begins to unpeel it. It spurts into his right eye. He winces.

When I return to the community section they are gone, but Trev is there, gently shaking the sleeping giant awake. It takes him several attempts. The man wakes, looks around him.

'Can't sleep here, friend.'

The man replies in Polish.

'Yeah,' Trev says. 'Well, no sleep here. You understand? No sleepy in library.'

The man smiles and nods his head, suggesting compliance. Trev touches the man's shoulder and returns to his office. The man falls immediately back to sleep.

Trev, having spotted him on CCTV, wearily troops back out again and shakes the man. He's in a deep, deep sleep. His right hand clutches his mobile phone. Trev finally manages to rouse him, but he won't be moved. A manager is radioed. It's rare for Facilities to call for back-up. I have to head upstairs for an hour in Nonfiction so don't witness the outcome.

Later, Trev talks me through it. 'So the manager comes down and the fellow still won't shift, so she leans down and grabs his mobile phone and takes it off him. This gets him up. She hands the phone to Derek [Facilities] and Derek leads him out of the library like a donkey, with his mobile phone. So, anyway, we're outside, me, the Polish bloke, Derek and the manager. The manager goes back in. Derek's just about to give the fellow his phone and he kicks out, catches Derek on the right nut.' Trev grabs the right-hand side of his testicles to demonstrate the precise place. 'So he goes to kick Derek again and I manage to grab his foot before he takes one of Derek's bollocks off. I say to the fellow, "That's assault, that is, I'm calling the police. You'd better wait here." So I'm calling them up on the mobile and the bloke legs it. Takes off. So I go after him. Derek's still nursing his nuts. Get through to the Old Bill. Explain what's happened (I'm running all this time) and tell them where we are. So we're not far from the main police station. Bloke doesn't know it but he's running in their direction. So, anyway, get to the street the station's on and I'm still on the phone. Running out of puff by now, but this car goes past and the driver pulls the wheel and the car swings round and blocks off the street. Two plain clothes coppers get out, grab the Pole. He fights. They get him on the bonnet, cuff him and take him away.'

'Result,' I say.

'Yes. Only they don't charge him.'

'Why not?'

'Because we took his phone off him. That's why. Shouldn't have done that. His property. Couldn't charge the fellow. So Derek's got a sore right bollock for nothing.'

Bookmark 5

Headed: 'Meal Planner'.

Monday – Veg Stir Fry

Tuesday – Pasta – butter

Wednesday – Cider-pot roasted pork belly, mash pot

Thursday – Same as Wed

Friday – Fish and chips (mush peas)

Sat – Chicken Curry (pops)

Valentime's Day

Trish and her friends are in today. Their usual space has been taken by a meeting of the Read Aloud group, so they have arrayed themselves on the single sofa and the floor beside the reservations shelves. Trish peels away. She's served by my colleague but calls over. "'Ello.'

'Hello, Trish.'

'Oh, it's you.'

'Yes. It's me.'

'It's Valentime's Day, you know.'

'Soon. Yes.'

'You married?'

'Yes. Are you sending any cards, Trish?'

'Oh yeah.'

'Who to?'

'Can't say. I've been watching that programme on the telly about that family what go and live in the wilderness. This looks like where they're living.' She holds up a flimsy book of jungle photographs, which is being issued to her by my colleague.

She pushes over two CDs: one by A-ha, the other by Kiss.

'Weren't here last week,' she says.

'No?' (She was.) 'Where were you?'

'Went to Spain.'

'Whereabouts?'

'The country. It was veh hot.'

'Did you all go?'

'What?'

'All of you?'

'Yes.'

She points to the Kiss CD. The band are, as always, in full monochrome face make-up, lengthy tongues protruding. 'Is he a cat?'

'Who?'

'Him?'

'Possibly.'

'Seed him on the telly. Do you know my carer?'

'Yes.'

'She's very nice. We're going out today.'

'Where to?'

'It's a surprise. It's very noisy where we are.'

'Have a good day, Trish.'

'Thank you. I like your hair.'

'Thank you, Trish.'

She returns to the group, opens the jungle book on her knee and invites the young man sitting next to her to look through it with her. I assume the man is one of the staff members. When she opens the first page, the young man says: 'Wow!' He repeats this with equal enthusiasm as she opens every subsequent page – thirty or forty times. Another of the group explains loudly how she had fallen over that morning and slightly bruised her knee. 'God!' the same young man says and punctuates her story by repeating the oath again and again and again.

Soon they are preparing to leave. One asks another: 'How long did it take to get your coat on?'

'About ten seconds.'

'It took me about forty-five. I timed it.'

Somebody calls out: 'Where's Peter?'

The others join the chorus. 'Peter! Peter!' One of the tribe has gone missing, causing mass panic. While they await his return I hear one of the carers in conversation with a young man. 'But how old do you think you are?' she asks him.

The young man contemplates: 'Two?'

'No, not two. How old are you, Glenda?' she calls out.

'What?'

'Glenda, how old are you?'

'In years?'

'Yes.'

'Twenty-three years.'

'Glenda is forty-six,' the carer says.

'Am I?' Glenda asks her.

'Yes, Glenda,' the carer turns back to the young man and repeats the question: 'So, Glenda's forty-six, how old do you think you are – because you're a bit younger, aren't you?'

The young man gives the question thought. 'Twenty-three?'

At which point Peter arrives from the Gents. His return is greeted with relief and calls of welcome from the group. He smiles and the crocodile is led out back to the minibus. As they leave they gleefully call and wave goodbye to the staff and customers.

SPRING

The Story of My Life

A long day in one of the community libraries on the edge of town. Thankfully this not one of the regular haunts of the Thin Man, Mr Jones. The library, along with a grim convenience store that sells undrinkable coffee from a machine, a post office and a chemist's, is at the centre of a sleepy estate established in the 1950s. It's an unremarkable outpost bordered by parched, chalky pastureland, parched, chalky sheep and barbed wire fences that act as washing lines for windblown fleece. The estate tends to be the first port of call for many of those moving into the area because property there is relatively affordable. The library is well used and, alongside the books, also has a collection of toys that can be borrowed. They are sanitised between each loan and then returned to a sealed plastic bag. The library opens three days a week and on Thursdays it closes at 7 p.m. During the quiet final hours of late opening at a community library, there are usually only a few customers at a loose end who wander in for a chat or to use the PCs.

It's my first day in this library so I'm unfamiliar with the clientele. The regular librarian seems to know them all by name. It's clear that they like him and respect him. Children are easy in his presence. He takes time to recommend books to them and knows which has played a significant game of football for the school or performed in a show.

At 5.20 three customers remain in the library. The smell of cooking wafts in through an open window from a close-by house – a pie, by the smell of it. The three customers are: a young man using a PC to print out his motor insurance certificate; a white-faced old man in a long coat with a small plastic bag gloving his right hand, making pencil notes in a spiral-bound notebook; and a hugely overweight boy in sports leisurewear using one of the Children's PCs. Earlier, the boy visited the counter and informed me that there were no buses coming out of town because they had closed the city centre. A woman had been stabbed and the police had cordoned off the area. I checked it out on the internet. This revealed that the woman had not been stabbed: she'd been hit by a bus and taken to the hospital, badly injured. I tell the boy this. The boy explains that the news must be wrong because, 'my mate saw the stabbing and the police ran after the man and got him . . . my mate saw it.'

A man walks in, talking loudly on his mobile phone. Clive is a late-fortysomething with a hawk-like stare. He has a good head of centre-parted hair worn slightly long and flecked with grey. He is wearing a blue cotton T-shirt over a paunch (he looks six months pregnant but, paunch aside, he is lean), khaki shorts, new trainers (budget) and black ankle-length socks. He is carrying a second mobile phone in his other hand along with a large bunch of keys.

'Yeah,' he says into his mobile, 'well, there's not much point me interviewing them and them leaving straight off. Half the time the interview is longer than they stay working for you.' His eyes slide towards the counter as his conversation continues – he's looking for an audience. I nod politely. He's found one.

There are six PCs in this library. The young man printing out his motor insurance is sitting at the one at the furthest end of the desk. Clive maintains eye contact with me as he moves to the PCs and then takes the seat next to the man. He continues his phone conversation, his eyes now straying to the other man's PC screen. Five minutes later the call is ended but, with barely a break, he engages the man next to him in a conversation about insurance.

'Yeah, I've been driving for twenty years,' Clive says in the tone of a young comedian embarking on an amusing anecdote. 'Never had an accident and I still pay three hundred quid a year. What's all that about?' He laughs. 'Eh?' I don't hear the man's reply. The monologue goes on. I tune out of it. After five minutes the other man makes an excuse and leaves hurriedly.

Clive wanders to the counter to collect a sheet of printing and introduces himself. I admit that this is my first visit to this particular library, but I know that I am irrelevant. All he needs is a willing pair of ears. At close range I see that Clive has the habit of watching for a response to every statement he makes before moving on to the next one – weighing its meaning by slightly squinting his eyes. This watchfulness adds weight to the image of him as a small bird of prey.

Clive's apparently had a bad day at work: 'It makes you laugh,' he begins, laughing. 'I've worked all my life and never been happy in a job. What's all that about?' He watches, waits, perfectly still, and my non-committal reply provides him with the permission he needs to begin a monologue that lasts for twenty minutes. It's exhausting to listen to. Between many of the statements his right hand delves into the pocket of his shorts and rearranges his genitals, suggesting that his anecdotes are being released from his testicles one at a time.

'I could write a book about my life . . .' Clive goes on. 'Yeah, things that have happened to me. I'd call it "The Story of My

213

Life". Listen to this: I live in a flat. Second floor. Man came round to fit a conservatory last week. I said he'd got the wrong place. He looked at his board and said he hadn't. I said he's welcome to try. He looked at me like it was my fault I lived on the second floor.

'My neighbour up the road, he's got my bed. I know he has. It was delivered to the wrong place three months ago and he never said anything but he's got it.'

Pause/stare/pause/continue.

'What else? Oh yeah, my phone. This'll make you laugh. My phone. I phone up BT to get a line installed, right? Take a day off work and they don't turn up. So I call them up and set up another day. Don't come again. Phone them. They say the phone's been connected. I say it hasn't. They say it has. It's been connected at the exchange. The line's been activated. I just have to plug the phone in. "Where?" I say. "Plug it in where?" "In the socket in the corner of the room," they say. "What socket?" I ask. "The one in the corner of the room." I tell them there isn't a socket in the corner of the room because they never turned up to put it in. That was why I was phoning. They say they'll have to log a fault. That's the only way they can get it in the system. "A fault on what?" I say. "On the socket." "But there isn't a socket," I tell them. They say they know that but it's the only way to get it into the system. I say, "OK, do what you need to do." Take another day off work. Man comes round and says, "Where's the fault?" I say the fault is that there's no socket. "What?" he says. "It's logged as a faulty socket." "Yeah," I say, "well, it was the only way to get it onto the system. You're welcome to look," I say. He looks round but he can't find one. No surprise there. Told him he wouldn't. So he puts one in. "Never seen anything like it," he said. Makes you laugh.'

Brief pause for breath.

'Oh yeah, my postman. He's been delivering for twenty years and he still can't get the right house.

'Everybody's angry nowadays. Traffic jam going into town. Man rolls down his window and asks me if it's this bad all the time. I say, "No, mate, usually it's worse."

'Rubbish skips, what's all that about? A while back they delivered a skip on the drive. It's still there three months later. The bin men can't get the bins out. Rubbish all over the place. Now we've got rats in and out of the place. Hundreds of them. I called the landlord. Said there was nothing he could do about it. I told him about the night storage heaters. Never been serviced. When you turn them on they smoke, I told him. That made him sit up. There's a heater on the wall in the bathroom. Electric. Hanging off. He came round. When we went in there, it fell off the wall. Straight up. I said, "I'm glad you were here to see that." He said he was too.

'Tell you something else. Like I said, I live in a flat. Wake up every day with two cats on my feet. Not mine. Don't know where they come from. Every day they're there. The other day there was a fox in there. I told him to get out. He went. Must have been English cause he understood me.'

He pauses briefly for breath and sniffs the air before looking around the room. He goes on – I sense he's running out of steam:

'There's history under here. I can feel it. I'm psychic, you know.

'Tell you something else. You know the bypass by the park? Yeah? Well, I was with a man and I was standing under it and I pointed up and I said, "You know what? I used to play up there." He looked at me and said, "What? On the dual carriageway?" I said, "No, it used to be fields. They drove a cutting through for the bypass." The Queen Mother opened the estate. Before my time that was.

'Oh yeah, history.

'You know something? I'll tell you this. A few years ago they had to call the Fire Brigade out to the Jobcentre. It's not there now, it's a Sainsbury's. Know which one I mean? Know why they called them out? There was a massive cabbage growing out of the drain on the roof. Massive. Bigger than your head. They put ladders up and cut it out.

'Anyway, I've got to go. Got things to do. Cheers.'

Prime Suspects

At the morning briefing there's an air of quiet reflection. Gloom, perhaps. The Doobie Brothers have accompanied the Van Box processing but even their sunny Californian stylings don't lighten the mood. The deadline for those volunteering for redundancy is five days away. Many of the long-serving staff have expressed interest in going. So many, in fact, that the concern now is that there might be too many opting for it and some won't be allowed to leave. Whatever the number, a huge amount of expertise will be lost overnight. The word is that those who will be allowed to go will leave at the end of the month. The team of casuals has been increased significantly, which suggests that the service will be maintained by them after the exodus. The longer-term plan is for casuals to be replaced by apprentices and, perhaps, volunteers.

The remaining branch libraries will be staffed by a single library officer instead of the customary two. A paper on single staffing has been drafted and circulated with security high on the agenda. The community libraries will become isolated outposts – but at least they will stay open. The underlying philosophy still seems to be to keep the buildings and minimise the staff costs in the hope that when the austerity measures end perhaps the libraries will bloom again – unlikely, I should think. Media commentators are now recognising that this is the biggest challenge the service has faced since its inception nearly 170 years ago.

Free public libraries grew out of the subscription library movement. In the late eighteenth century, a predominantly agrarian society in which learning was handed down from generation to generation became a predominantly industrial society in which up-to-date information was needed by a new breed of tradesmen and artisans. One of the first establishments to service this need was the 'Economical Library', established in 1797 in Kendal, providing books for a cheap subscription. An 'Artizan's Library' opened two years later in Birmingham. The Mechanics' Institutes movement was one of the most forward-thinking in this respect in the level of provision for its members. D. H. Lawrence often acknowledged his debt to the small collection of fiction at the library of the Eastwood Mechanics' Institute when he was young (Eastwood Library in Nottinghamshire holds a mass of material on Lawrence and is part of the D. H. Lawrence heritage trail). The Mechanics' Institutes' libraries and the other workers' libraries demonstrated what form a national public library might take.

As the appetite for such a service grew, William Ewart, a Radical MP, and a cataloguer at the British Museum Library called Edward Edwards (whose parents could perhaps have benefitted from borrowing a library book on naming children) campaigned for legislation to allow municipalities to provide public libraries. The Public Libraries Acts of 1850 and 1853 were the result but were flawed, not least because they limited the funds that could be devoted to libraries and initially even failed to provide the right to pay for the acquisition of books. As a result, fewer than fifty communities took advantage of the

Acts over the following twenty years. The legislation, though, went through various amendments and by the turn of the century around 500 towns had library services. Fiction and other popular reading material was treated with suspicion by the emerging middle classes and many of the earlier institutions concentrated their spending on that which would educate rather than entertain their members.

Two main factors had influenced the growth in libraries. The first was donations by benefactors such as the Scottish-American industrialist Andrew Carnegie, which improved the housing of the collections and raised their public profile. The second was the emergence of a library profession. Melvil and others paved the way in the USA. In the UK librarians such as James Duff Brown, Stanley Jast and Ernest Savage led the way in their own libraries, trained younger librarians and wrote on professional matters. Eventually legislators, councillors, fellow librarians and the public caught up with them.

But until the cuts bite the libraries continue to serve all who come through the doors. This being Monday, the Travelling Man is among the first in when the doors open. He spots me and makes a beeline for the counter. As always, he leans his stick against the desk and, as he catches his breath, apologises for disturbing me. We exchange the usual morning platitudes and then he explains that he's looking for the new Lynda La Plante. He can't remember the title but knows it's a single word. I look it up for him.

'*Tennison*,' I tell him. 'Prequel to *Prime Suspect*.'

'That's it!' he says with huge delight. 'S'funny, I like La Plante. I know that world and she knows it too . . .'

I wait, knowing from experience we're going back into the past. His eyes lose focus. He looks over my shoulder and sees himself as a younger man. He would have been good-looking: cheeky, well dressed (he still is), sparkling blue eyes – women would have liked him for his charm and easy laugh – a man with a boyish enthusiasm for the world. One of the skills he still has is to know how to make people feel valued even though he tends to prefer the centre stage. It's a rare talent.

He begins: 'I had a friend, good mate. He was a silversmith, but he loved his motors. We used to go out, me and him, dancing, drinking. Seventeen, eighteen. Always used to walk home. I lived in Chelsea, he lived in Fulham; different manor. Long walk from the West End. Anyway, one night we was out and walking back, about – I don't know, it was about half-two, three-ish. We were on Park Lane. For some reason we were walking down the centre of it, on the raised grass. He said, "Wait there." We was near the Dorchester. Just over the road. All lit up. Anyway, he goes off. Next thing I know is this red MG's pulled up. It's him. He spotted it outside the Dorchester. Took me home in it. Roy, was it? That's right, maybe Roy. Silversmith he was. Anyway, he loved racing cars. He wasn't a proper villain, not violent, just loved the cars. We were young. He made a name for himself a few years later. Biggs knew him. Took him on for a job. He was the main getaway driver for the Great Train Robbers.'

'Really?'

'No word of a lie. He got thirty years. But he came from a different manor. Funny thing, if you walked into a pub they knew straight away. Even if the pub was full. They knew if you were off your manor . . . One night I went into a club and this man – Johnny, his name was – very tall, about six foot six, black fellow, he's looking for somebody. I go out of the club and he grabs me and lifts me off my feet. Well, I'm only a little fellow as you can see. He lifts me off my feet and he puts a gun – a pistol – to my throat. Straight up. He does. And he asks me where this fellow, whatsisname, is. I tell him, "I don't know, honest, Johnny." He lets me go. Next night I'm in a pub. Walk in and Johnny's there. He says, "Here he is!" And he waves me over and buys me a drink. There were always fights in those places. Always over women. They loved it. Thing is, the men were stood at the bar and the birds sat down together and you never knew who was with who. One night I asked a girl if I could walk her to the tube. Went past a doorway and this bloke jumped me. Her fellow. She never told me! Anyway I legged it.'

'Which were the worst manors?'

'Oh, East End. East End. Working-class areas – Krays and that lot. And Battersea. They were the worst.'

By now somebody is waiting to be served. The new La Plante is ordered, the Travelling Man walks off without a goodbye, returns for his stick, retrieves it and then goes to sit down.

Curiosity piqued, in a quiet moment I look up the Great Train Robbers on the internet and there I find a photo of Roy John James aka 'Weasel'. The text confirms that he was, indeed, the main getaway driver – and also a silversmith. The single fingerprint he left at the gang's farmhouse hideaway led the police to him and he was caught after a rooftop chase. He had planned to invest his share of the spoils in new car technology. After serving twelve years of his thirty-year sentence he returned to selling silver before moving to Spain.

In 1993 he was jailed again for shooting his wife's father and died soon after leaving prison, aged sixty-two.

Print Disability

Just before lunch I take the opportunity to visit the Gents. The small room is crowded. Three men are leaning against the sinks waiting to use the single cubicle. The man at the front of the queue calls out: 'How long you going to be? You've been in there for ten minutes.'

A short pause, then the reply: 'You got a stopwatch?'

'I need a crap.'

'There's another toilet upstairs.'

The man spots my nametag and whispers: 'He's up to something.'

I kneel and see that the view under the cubicle is blocked by a black canvas bag. Outside the Gents I encounter Stef from Facilities. I explain the situation.

'Shooting up,' she surmises. 'He got sunglasses on?'

'I don't know. All I know is that he has a black bag.'

She's just spotted a man in sunglasses walking quickly away from the Gents. He's carrying a black holdall. She follows him, but he's out of the library before she can reach him.

Facilities are on high alert. On Saturday, a spray of blood was found decorating the lavatory wall. A user was spotted leaving the Gents with a hypodermic needle in his hand, fully loaded. He was ushered out of the building with caution by Facilities.

At lunch today, the team are discussing what would happen if the hypodermic had been discharged into one of them. The consensus was that it was not something they'd particularly relish but their major concern would be whether the needle was dirty. A pause, and then one of them offers a recent experience: two young men were together in the cubicle. This raised suspicion with a member of the public, who alerted Security. They found the boys shooting up and tried to lead them out of the building. The boys protested loudly at their treatment and started 'kicking off'. As they crossed the library floor several members of the public used their phones to take photos of the incident, complaining at the treatment meted out by Security to the poor, innocent lads. The story is greeted by silence by the others. Nothing new there.

In Children's immediately after the lunch break, it strikes me that if anyone wanted to study human behaviour this would be the place to do it. A grandfather – elderly, possibly Greek – is standing above a child who is crawling along the rug. He's peering down at the child as if he's standing on thin ice and is waiting for the ice to crack and the child to fall through. His wife is also watching the child fondly, just within reach. Should the ice break, she would be the one who would dive in to retrieve her grandson. A younger grandfather is on the mat playing with a toddler. A sleep-deprived woman is asleep with her baby on her lap. She has already been to the counter to ask for a book on how to get your child to sleep through the night. At a table scattered with crumbs, peel, fruit, berries, nuts and other assorted grains and low-fat, low-salt snacks, a hugely pregnant woman is watching her child audition the food by inserting it a short distance between her lips. The food that passes the test is shoved firmly in and chewed. The rejected food is spat out onto the table, some of it bouncing onto the floor, where it remains uncollected. A crawler has escaped and is moving rapidly towards Fiction. She knows she is being tailed by her mother who, for a while, allows her freedom but eventually scoops her up, lifts her high, buries her face in her tiny midriff, blows a raspberry, and the child laughs in delight. Another child is having a temper tantrum. Her body is rigid as she screams. Her mother watches, calmly waiting for the storm to pass. The quietest, least animated adult in there is a worried-looking young man with a seven- or eight-month baby son. The boy is sitting on the carpet at the man's feet. I realise that the man is the only adult in the room who has not smiled. Children's is a place of harvested smiles. The rest of the library is like the world outside: a place of neutral, often worried, faces.

The afternoon's second customer has silver-dyed hair, which is blue at the ends as if she has dipped it into an inkwell. She is probably in her forties, with purple-rimmed glasses and a badge on her striped oversized cardigan which says 'Ask me if you need help'. Her cheeks are rouged. Her card has not been recognised at the automatic issues/returns machine and she wants me to issue her two books. One is on the care of hamsters, the other on guinea pigs. She's polite, undemanding of attention, but looks like she'd welcome a chat.

'Do you have a hamster?' I try.

'No, I'm thinking of getting one. Or a guinea pig. For the company.'

'Good idea.'

'Which one do you think would be best?'

'Depends what you're looking for. Guinea pigs are more sedentary, but hamsters don't make as much mess.' I speak from long experience.

'I'm looking for one that would sit on my knee. While I'm watching the television.'

I tell her that from experience, both would serve the purpose, although chances are that the guinea pig would make regular deposits on her clothing, while the hamster would be flightier, refusing to stay still for any length of time. She ponders and tells me that she intends to give whichever she opts for the run of the bathroom floor for exercise. 'I have lino in there,' she says, 'but there are carpet tiles in the living room and I don't want them to start smelling.'

I wish her luck with her decision. She laughs, suggests that I think she must be a little eccentric, if not mad. I assure her that she seems quite normal to me, which she is in the terms of the clientele of the library.

A woman arrives at the counter. She immediately explains that she's had one cataract done but wonders why there's applause from the front of the library because she can't quite see what's going on. The question is tagged on to the revelation as though the two are in some way part of the same thought. I explain that the applause is from the audience at the launch of the Mood Boosting books scheme for children. Local primary schoolchildren between the ages of nine and eleven have been canvassed on which books cheer them up and a list has been prepared. Inevitably Roald Dahl, Jacqueline Wilson and J. K. Rowling feature, but so do some more obscure authors – Ryan North and Cathy Cassidy. Noir writer Jo Nesbø makes a surprise appearance with *Doctor Proctor's Fart Powder*.

The woman is uninterested in the initiative and repeats that her eyes are bad and goes on to tell me she has trouble with her television. 'It keeps saying "no signal", so I phone up India. They're terribly helpful but they tell me to switch the box off and then back on. So I try but quite often it doesn't work. The problem is that the remote controller is on the coffee table and the cat sits on it and presses the buttons and I don't know which ones she's pressed.'

I suggest changing her membership to Adult Print disability. This will give her free access to audiobooks. She accepts the offer but says she's wary about putting a CD in the slot in her TV. I explain that it would be better to put it into her CD player – the TV slot is for DVDs. She doesn't have a CD player, she tells me. She did, but the cat broke it.

I watch an elderly woman as she rests, trying to draw in breath, on one of the triangular comfy seats in Fiction. She is very, very old, but has made it to the library. She looks unwell. Her face is grey, her skin is wrinkled. Her knuckles, visible on the claw of a hand that grasps her walking stick, are the size of golf balls. Her walking stick is a matt grey colour with a triangular support at the base. She seems to need help but just as I am about to offer it, her husband arrives, walking slowly along the aisle (Fiction, M). She tries to raise her head because perhaps she senses him, but even that seems beyond her. He is as old as she is, older perhaps. His face brightens when he sees her. 'OK, darling?' he asks her. She manages a smile and they walk out together, slowly, arm-in-arm. Their pride in each other; their love; their support of each other shouts silently across the room.

It's a long shift. Nine until seven. Between 5 and 6 p.m. I am upstairs in Nonfiction. The three rooms are full of people studying. I wander around and count them: 114 silent people.

In the final hour of late opening many of the more conventional customers leave and the more eccentric ones, undiluted by the normals, become more visible. I spot the Thin Man at a computer. Mr Jones' latest community ban does not extend to the main library and he's recently taken to coming in most days. He knows who I am, and demonstrates this not with a 'hello' but by odd, slightly threatening suggestions. Today, he looks down at my sandals and suggests that they're similar to the ones his female solicitor wears. He tells me he's taken her to task for it, considering them inappropriate. He's wearing a white, V-necked T-shirt, combat trousers and dayglo green training shoes. When I pass him he's looking up the weather on the internet. His eyes slide in my direction then shift quickly back to the screen.

It's been a long day and I'm heading to the Gents for a few moments' peace. A middle-aged woman in high heels, a short black skirt and scoop-necked T-shirt accosts me just as I'm about to open the door.

''Scuse me, darling. You do work here, don't you?'

'Yes.'

She is very drunk. The words are slurred. She has a drinker's pallor. Behind her is her Lolita daughter in full make-up, bright red lips, defined cheekbones, skin-tight white jeans, reading a message on her spangled pink iPhone.

The woman goes on: '. . . Atkinson.' It's the only word I can make out. 'Oh,' she says, 'ova there.' She heads off towards the A shelving. I make it to the sanctuary of the Gents, where I find Brewer packing his bag for the night, stealing what remains of the toilet paper, emptying his pockets of detritus into the toilet bowl, patting himself down and talking to himself.

Back at the counter the drunk woman returns, waving her arms in the air. She points to a stack of books being carried by her daughter. 'I don't know what to do with them,' she calls as if her daughter has just found an unexploded bomb and is looking for somewhere it can be detonated safely.

I issue her daughter's books, and then the three Val McDermid books the woman is taking out. She weaves out of the library, her daughter in tow, back on her pink mobile phone, zookeeper to the unpredictable, slightly dangerous creature leading the way.

The tannoy bing-bongs and the recorded announcement is played out. 'The library is now closed. Please make your way immediately to the exit.'

On my way home I see Brewer making his nest in the door-way of a small jewellery shop. Rain is beginning to fall.

The Other Side

I'm working on the other side of the city today and, as always, travel there on my Vespa. Another storm has ravaged Europe. The roads are slick with water and oil – but the journey is only four miles. I reflect on the fifty-five miles I used to travel each way on my scooter when I worked in London and I'm thankful.

It's the day after the formal announcements have been made about the proposed changes to the service – i.e. the cuts. One is for single staff working at the branch libraries. There have always been at least two, on grounds of safety. A working paper has been drafted with safety at the top of the list. The morning conversation inevitably revolves around the new proposals. A female library officer who works at one of the outposts is adamant that she will not work alone – for anything. I ask her why and she brings up the name of the Thin Man. He was a regular at the library where she worked.

'It's all right if he doesn't single you out,' she tells me. 'But he singled me out. He used to follow me upstairs on the bus. I'm not going to work alone.'

It's pouring with rain. Customers and books arrive saturated. A man, dripping, comes up to the desk with a large plastic bag.

'Need to cancel my booking tomorrow. I've got two hours. Looking for a job. Got to cancel, we're missing an Allen key.'

The information hangs there. 'PC 12, IT Suite. Twelve o'clock. PC 12.'

He's a large-bellied man, talking very loudly. He has a badge sewn roughly onto his woollen jumper. The badge is around three inches square and is a red rose. He is wearing a soaked woollen bobble hat, soaked denims and soaked orange training shoes.

'Yes,' he goes on. 'So this table came for my brother with screws. Needed to assemble it but there's no Allen key so I need to get it from my father's this afternoon and go round tomorrow to put up the table.'

'They sell them at Bolts and Things a few doors down,' I tell the man.

'Yes, but my father has lots of them. If I buy one then I'll have no use for it after that 'cause I can borrow my father's.'

I cancel the PC booking.

'My brother's special needs. He lives on his own. I treat him normal. That's best. My father treats him like a flower cause he's special. He's a diabetic, my father. So my brother phones up and tells me to come round. He wants me to go round straight away. I tell him I can't go round straight away because I've only had one meal today – and that was orange juice – and my dad can't go round because he's diabetic and he needs his meals regular. So I go round after I've had a sandwich and he shows me the table but the Allen key is missing. There's a bubble in the wrapping – a blister thing – where it should be but it's fallen out. The screws are there but the Allen key is missing, so I phone my father and he tells me I shouldn't buy one because he's got them indoors so I'm going round to get it. That's why I need to cancel my booking.'

As he leaves, he shouts something from the door but I can't make out what it is. Facilities Trev wanders over and asks if the man was having a go at me about something. He's been watching from a distance, sensing I might be in trouble. From the tone of his voice he said the man sounded very angry. I tell him he wasn't complaining or particularly angry, it was an informational conversation about a missing Allen key. Trev begins to wander away again.

'I can give you further details if you like,' I offer.

'No need,' he says. 'You know you can get Allen keys from Bolts and Things?'

I tell him that I do.

I see a girl – a woman, perhaps seventeen, perhaps twenty-five, sitting at a PC. I did not see her come in with her mother. Her mother comes to the desk. She is in her fifties.

'We're at the ... we're trying to get a ... a thing ... you know a ... thing,' she says.

'You're on a computer?'

'That's right.'

'And you want to print something?'

'That's right! I want to print something. Just a page. It's my daughter.'

In the far corner of the room her daughter is transfixed by the screen. She is pale, thin, delicate; a Henry James ghost. Her eyes seem to be staring into another world.

I approach her carefully from behind and ask if I can help.

'Yes,' she says but doesn't move. I reach around her for the mouse and smell cigarette smoke on her thin coat and an out-of-time perfume. I print the document, go to the printer, retrieve it. It's a question and answer; a health one. The question is 'What is the difference between bipolar disorder and schizophrenia or schizoaffective disorder?' The paper suggests that a bipolar sufferer will have moments of normality between the psychotic and depressive episodes. With schizophrenia the psychosis is present all the time.

I give the sheet of paper to the girl. She thanks me and then logs out and then she and her mother leave.

At 3.30 I'm surprised to see that the Allen key man is making his way back to the counter.

'I need to rebook my PC for tomorrow,' he tells me.

'You found an Allen key?' I ask him.

'Yes!' he says. 'You were paying attention!'

'How did you get hold of one?'

'Caretaker had one. Job done. I took some pictures for my father.'

Before I can ask, he's unsheathed his phone from the holster around his waist and is displaying an image of a small bedsit – incredibly neat, with a tube-framed, smoked glass-topped table at the centre of the room, and two chairs. Beneath them is a rug emblazoned with the badge of the local football team; behind that, a small, pristine kitchenette. The washing machine is brand new and still has its triangular energy consumption sticker on it. His brother stands on the rug, staring at the floor. He's large, shaven-headed and inert and looks like a post-breakdown Syd Barrett.

I rebook the session for tomorrow and Alan leaves, explaining that after his session here he's having lunch with his father. I wish him well.

Getting Old

The Travelling Man comes to sit at the counter, leans his stick against it and asks me to look up a Colm Tóibín book. Today he doesn't seem to know me. He begins an anecdote but it tails off with a '. . . Sorry, can't remember. It's my memory. It's going. I used to travel, but when my memory started going, I lost confidence. Couldn't remember which airport . . . Alzheimer's.' For the first time he's named his condition. The impending loss of who he is, the delayed loss of who he was. He's looking for *Brooklyn*. He's just seen mention of it in the *Sunday Times*, which he has been reading in the library because, he confesses, he's too mean to buy papers nowadays. The system suggests we have two copies on the shelf. I tell the Travelling Man to rest while I hunt it down, and, remarkably, the two copies are actually on the shelf – hardback and paperback. I bring both back.

'That's the one!' He opts for the hardback. I issue it but the system reports that he's had the book out before in 2011. His enthusiasm immediately extinguishes, but he opts to take the book anyway.

'You know I saw a film last week. The new one with Michael Caine in it. I thought, f*** me, he looks old, and then I thought, hold on, I'm the same age!' I tell him the thought is a familiar one to me.

We've been launched into the past again. His mind ranges over his old manor: Chelsea, the bridge, Sloane Square, World's End, bombed-out London, hiding on the top of buses so he could roam the city as a kiddie, happier days, the brighter colours of childhood. I prepare for a familiar anecdote but suddenly he's found focus and seems to know me again. He looks over his shoulder to check there's nobody waiting. There isn't.

'Let me tell you something. I'll be quick.'

'That's fine.'

'I used to live in Chelsea. You know that.'

'Yes.'

'So at this time, probably I was about . . . twenty-four? I went over to Jersey. Lots of us went over there because we heard the booze was cheap and people said you could have a good time in the clubs. Anyway, I went over there and I got a job on the deckchairs. On the beach. I loved it. F***ing loved it! . . . So, anyway, there was this girl, well, this woman, and she was . . . she was beautiful, and I asked her if she wanted to meet me for a drink, you know, at the end of the day, and she said yes. So that night I meet her and we go to this club and this fellow comes up to me and says, "Do you know she's Billy Bridge's bird?" I say, "What?" He says, "Straight up, she's Bridge's." I go, "F*** me," and I run out. I run out! 'Cause Billy Bridge is a villain. A real villain. So anyway . . .' He checks over his shoulder again. Thankfully there is nobody in the queue. He drops his voice a little, leans closer. 'So anyway, two weeks later, I'm on the beach and the girl's there again and she's with a bloke and it's Billy Bridge. He's come over to see her. So I lie low. He doesn't see me and neither does she. Two or three days later there's a jewellery robbery in Saint Helier. And I know it's Bridge. Local police don't, but I do. No question whatsoever. So I've got this friend over there. Pam. Good-looking woman. Model. She's tall, very skinny. I'm short, so we were just friends, but she knows Billy and his lot. So I see her and she's got, you know, tits. Turns out that Billy's given her the jewels to get back home, on the ferry, and she's stuffed them down her bra. Straight up. That's absolutely true. She's never had tits before. And she's proud of them . . .'

He's back on track now. Back in gear.

'One more. Just one more . . . So this pub, just behind Sloane Square, I go in there drinking. And there's a lot of money round there: Chelsea. Posh people with money, but that's all right because I get on with them and they get on with me. I can talk to anybody. We mucked in together then. Not like now. So one night this bloke comes in, posh gent type. I knew him quite well, he used to live three doors down from the pub. Good-looking fellow. Good-looking wife, but they was always rowing. Big drinkers. Big rows in the pub. So I'm standing at the bar and I ask him how he is because he looks a bit rough and he says, "I've just killed my wife." I go: "What!" I think he's joking, but he's not. He's just killed his wife at home after a row and he's come straight to the pub. Anyway, he has a drink, then another and then he goes. And I hear that after that he went down to the south coast and some of his friends managed to get him over to France in a boat. But they caught him eventually and brought him back . . .'

'I'm sorry,' I say, looking over the Travelling Man's shoulder, where a man is waiting patiently to be served.

'God! Listen to me. I'm sorry,' the Travelling Man says. 'Sorry!' he calls to the young man. The young man smiles. He's in no rush. The Travelling Man leaves. His walking stick remains propped at the desk. I wait, but he doesn't change course to retrieve it as he heads for the door despite the fact that he is walking with some difficulty. I apologise to the customer who has just taken the seat at the desk and return the Travelling Man's walking stick to him. He recognises the stick, but doesn't seem to know me.

Bookmark 6

Today, the bookmark that falls from the pages of *Cider with Rosie* is literally an old bookmark. On one side is a competent watercolour of a vase of violet flowers, on the other is written:

Dearest Jugs,

Hope you had a lovely birthday. Sorry wasn't there on the day but had to take advantage of the Tommy courier service. Pressie is not in the same league as mine from you this year but hope you like it.

Lots of love, Juicy xxxx

The Amazon Habit

Australian psychedelic rock band Tame Impala accompany the morning's stock processing. The jaunty bass line bounces around the Fiction section. Time is accelerating. It seems like a day since Trish was in. It's actually been a week. I find her ferreting around the CD racks.

'Morning, Trish.'

'Oh, 'ello. I know you, don' I?'

'Yes.' (Etc.)

Trish takes a CD from the rack at random. 'Who's him?'

'Who?'

'Him.' She points at Gladys Knight. The Pips are in line behind her: cheesy grins, white shirts, afros and wide-lapelled red suits.

'Gladys Knight.'

'Is he good?'

'Yes, he's good.'

'I might get that.'

'You'll like it.'

Trish sets off for the counter, where one of the good-looking young male members of staff is working. She launches a bright seductive smile.

''Ello.'

'Hello,' he says.

'What you doing tonight?'

'I'm working late. Then I'm out.'

'Oh. You married?'

'Living with someone.'

The next woman is in a tangle. She's come in to reserve the new Joan Bakewell, *Stop the Clocks*. It's arrived from the wholesaler but not quite made it to the shelves. She's heard it on Radio 4. Many of the reservations are provoked by a mention on Radio 4. She's a gentle woman, extremely polite. Kind. Very kind. Her name might be Violet. She's struggling. She can't get her book into her bag. She can't get her card back into her purse. I volunteer to help her.

'It's sticks and gloves,' she says. 'Sticks and gloves.' Her thin leather gloves are caught around the leather strap on her walking stick, which is snagged tight around her wrist. Her hands are frozen with arthritis. Together we manage to get the returns out of her bag – a Virginia Woolf and a Georges Simenon.

Tomorrow, there's a meeting of the finance committee to dictate policy about those who have expressed an interest in redundancy. The full-timers are wary, flat – one declares himself, 'Very sad, but glad not to be around to see the service.' Another can't wait. He has a clock on his mobile that is counting down the hours. The mood of the rest fluctuates. One or two have found jobs but the general feeling is that they have no transferrable skills – patently untrue but symptomatic of a workforce under threat. News arrives of the opening of a refurbished volunteer-run library in Market Deeping, which was closed when the council withdrew funding. The library will have one paid librarian and a team of volunteers. The library is expected to open for three days a week at first, but the group behind it hope to extend it to six. One of the people behind the scheme suggests 'a library is a bedrock of civilisation'.

For some reason this prompts a memory of a time when my books were to be found on the shelves of a library, even if only for a short time around publication. Writers are addicts. One of their addictions is to hunt for their books on library shelves. The second is the Amazon habit. The advent of the 'Amazon sales ranking' has cost more productive hours at the typeface than writer's block or alcohol dependency. When a book is due to come out you'll find yourself listed, with a six-figure ranking. If the book is pre-ordered your ranking suddenly shoots up. You can hit the top two hundred with a few pre-orders. Anything more significant in terms of sales can get you close to the top twenty. It doesn't take much to move you up the charts, until you hit the top thirty or so when you need real sales to propel you towards number one. Once in the top twenty your chances of decent sales increase because your book becomes more visible. It's talked about – you might get invited onto Andrew Marr to bang on about the papers. You might get onto Radio 4 or to sit on the sofa on *The One Show*. But what really costs the time is the fact the sales rank changes on an hourly basis. The closest I got to the Toppermost of the Poppermost was 101 for a couple of hours in 1995 with my novel *Newton's Swing*. After that, for a few years, I actually sold fewer books than non-published authors by dint of the returns that were coming back into the warehouses of my publishers. My annual sales were in minus figures.

Incidentally, one library authority has just announced that it is putting a link to Amazon on its online catalogue, which means that if a customer can't find a book in the library's stock then, with one click, they can buy it and have it delivered to their house within a couple of days. Amazon have meanwhile announced they're going to try out deliveries using drones, which means that customers who can't find a book they want on the shelf can possibly have it parachuted into their patio within a couple of hours for a few quid. This has, needless to say, provoked a good deal of debate within the library community.

The third writer's addiction involves visiting bookshops around the publication date and moving your books into a more visible position on the shop floor – this, of course, is contingent on the bookshop actually stocking your books.

Today, I'm faced with a man who, after some preamble, admits that he is a writer and asks me to look up one of his books to see if it's in stock. It's a biography of a fairly famous British film star of the 1940s and 1950s. I admire his nerve. He's not even pretending he's somebody else but he tells me he's been in television for much of his life so he has that confidence and easy charm. He's dressed well, in a good tweed jacket, a nice scarf, decently cut jeans, and woollen beanie hat. He's probably in his sixties but he's worn well and he is chewing gum, which suggests that he still has his own teeth. Gum chewing by the over-sixties is rare. Sadly, the man's book is not in the library stock, neither is the next one he mentions or, indeed, the final one.

'Ah well,' he says, smiling.

I ask him about his TV career and he tells me that he's spent much of his life as a television producer, working with one of the leading lights of light entertainment for twenty or so years. The entertainer has now retired from the spotlight but the producer tells me he still calls him most days. They were very close. The entertainer's wife liked the producer and treated him in the same way she treated her husband. If they were going out to a ritzy awards ceremony she'd lay out two suits, one for each of them.

'Then I went insane,' he says. 'Technically insane.'

'Yes?'

'I had a car accident. It displaced my brain. I didn't know where I was for a few weeks. But I went to work. It was television, you see, insanity is tolerated. Encouraged, even. I don't quite know how I got away with it really. But . . . he was good to me. Once I was sitting in my flat talking to a woman, a writer, who had visited me. You know her, I'm sure.'

He mentions her name. I do, indeed, know her.

'Anyway, we were sitting there drinking tea and I suddenly forgot who she was; what she was doing there, so I phoned ***** up and said, "There's a strange woman in my living room." He asked me to describe her to him, which I did, and he told me who she was. Then I remembered and the conversation went on.'

He pauses, remembering his old friend, the entertainer. 'I was a producer, not a director, and I didn't much care for the gallery. I used to watch him from the flats at the side of the stage. I've never known anybody who had that connection with an audience. Nobody.'

I ask how the entertainer survives now that he's out of the public eye.

'Oh, he's OK. He's a working-class boy, like me. Working-class boys of my generation don't have debts. We don't go overdrawn. He was always careful with his money. Ah well . . .'

He asks for my name and says he will hunt down one of my novels to read. I wish him luck. We shake hands and he leaves.

But like the Travelling Man, today I'm mired in the past and remembering a few years ago when I was involved with a group of writers who met on a monthly basis in a dismal chilly room over a dire west London pub. We were all published, among us were some fairly well established (if fading) names. I went along expecting sparkling conversation and came away depressed by the litany of whinging over advances, agents, television people, the lack of interest from the film industry, etc., but still I went back each month. One elderly woman novelist always spent the evening complaining she couldn't get decent typewriter ribbons nowadays. This always provoked the anti-computer chorus; the technophobes who all seemed to write on old Amstrad computers and couldn't work out why they kept losing their works-in-progress when the device crashed.

The saddest thing to witness (apart from the charity-shop clothing) was the way in which these impoverished individuals scuttled to the bar on their way in, careful not to meet anybody's eye, then pretended to notice the group only as they brought over their cheap glass of house red wine, which they would then nurse for the next three hours. Nobody took the risk of going to the bar in case they had to buy a round. Anybody who did strike gold tended to come to one further meeting to brag about it, then disappear (presumably to Hollywood) never to be seen again. At 10.30 p.m. there was a mass exodus to the tubes to the far reaches of the capital or the unfashionable resorts of the south coast (many seemed to live in Hastings). The life of a mid-list writer is not a happy one.

I may re-join the group if they haven't all perished from hypothermia.

Happy Days

The two men have stepped out of a Samuel Beckett play. Beckett now seems eerily prescient given the current condition of the welfare state although his dustbin dwellers were presumably intended to be read metaphorically. I did, however, see two street drinkers yesterday shouting at a third, who was leaning into the mouth of a waste hopper, rummaging for something – 'Here! Get out of our house,' one of them called. I think this was done ironically, but nothing surprises nowadays. The street drinkers are proliferating – a can of Tennent's Extra or Diamond White in someone's grubby mitt mid-morning no longer being greeted by surprise by passers-by.

A shrine has recently been established where the city centre's drinkers now congregate to brag and strut and argue. On the graffitoed council wall that provides their backdrop there are a couple of dozen photocopied photographs of their fallen comrades – all of whom have perished in the cold. The dominant graffiti image is that of a large-eyed young girl crying ultramarine blue tears. There's also a jam jar with some plastic daffodils in it and a few dozen faded Post-its with messages on it. One of them reads: 'Thanks for your existence'. Another says, 'What will we do next time round? Where will we be? Miss you, Rudy. X'

Spring

The two men entering the library are regulars. There are no obvious clues as to what the relationship between them is – but something does tie them together because they are never seen apart. One is thin, early seventies, fairly short, and always wears a tweed, knee-length coat. Beneath it he sports a tie and a white shirt. He's built like Steptoe. His white hair is sparse and razored close to his skull. His long face has no fat on it. His eyes struggle to find focus and he seems perpetually to be trying to see something in the far distance. The man he comes in with, usually trailing a couple of steps behind him, is an old-fashioned bruiser. He has the face of an angry bulldog. He's in his late sixties and wears a donkey jacket and drainpipe denims with lengthy turn-ups. On his feet, steel toe-capped boots. His hair is greying but plentiful, dragged fiercely back from his forehead and held in place with gel. The sides of it are razored, the razored hair tapering down each side of his face into long Victorian sideburns.

Bulldog is bullying and dominant. He snaps terse instructions to the quiet man, who reacts to them with deference. I don't think they are a couple. But they are thieves.

Bulldog wears a black duffel bag; Navy surplus, not a flimsy fashion accessory. It's strapped on his back, the thick black rope across his chest. Inside it are three or four empty plastic litre bottles. Their destination is the water fountain. When they reach it, the Quiet Man stands guard, shielding Bulldog as well as he can given the relative disparities in their size. Bulldog, meanwhile, back to the room, fills the empty plastic bottles from the water fountain.

Facilities Bob knows them well. He watches them on his CCTV and when they come in, he stands behind a pillar and chuckles. I join him and ask him why he's laughing.

'They think it's mineral water. It's not. Comes straight from the tap, but it is chilled.'

Bottles filled, Bulldog leads the way out of the library and back to their gaff. I try to picture it: a damp basement bedsit, a small kitchenette with a two-ringed gas burner on the stainless-steel sink. Two upturned mugs. A Formica-topped table, a Sarson's vinegar bottle and salt and pepper pots lifted from the local café. A cat-litter tray. The sound of their upstairs bedridden neighbour coughing her guts up. Two armchairs, greasy at the headrest, angled towards the large, old-fashioned television. A tin brewery ashtray on the arm of one of them. A fruit bowl containing two black bananas. A grandfather clock woodenly ticking the seconds away. Two dozen empty plastic bottles queuing neatly in the hallway, waiting to be filled.

Happy Days.

The Gorilla in the Roses

'Aye, aye, it's the Spice boys,' Facilities Trev announces.

I look up from the book I'm reading at the main desk in Nonfiction – Robert Hughes' *Lucian Freud: Paintings*. It's post lunch and I'm trying to keep my head down for ten minutes. A stomach bug has laid me low for a week. When I explain to Trev why I'd been away, adding the fact that I lost three-quarters of a stone in a week, he says, 'That's nothing.'

'No?'

'Went into hospital three years ago for my guts and they gave me some powder to clear me out. Know what?'

'What?'

'Lost a stone. A stone! In three hours. Never left the toilet.'

'Nice.'

Trev returns to watching the two wild-eyed louts staggering from the Gents and weaving a jagged course towards the doors.

'Spice boys. Here we come,' he says.

'What?'

'Spice. Legal high. Not heard of it?'

I admit that there's a large gap in my knowledge when it comes to legal highs.

'Nasty stuff.'

'How do you take it?'

'Smoke it.' The louts have reached the door. One pushes the other – he collides against the wall, laughing. 'Read about it . . .' Trev clocks a young Mexican man. 'What's he doing? He's been here all day, just wandering around.' Trev sets off after him.

I look up 'Spice – Legal high'. It's a cannabis substitute. In 2009 the UK banned 'Cannabinoids', categorising them as Class B drugs, but the manufacturers keep one step ahead of the authorities by bringing new products to the market as the existing ones are added to the list. It's becoming a major trigger of violence in prisons. People are throwing it over the prison walls in tennis balls.

I return to Lucian Freud's world but look up when a shadow is cast over the page to see a middle-aged man in a too-small denim jacket and tartan shirt looking down at one of the images. He is unshaven and looks like he hasn't slept for weeks but undoubtedly belongs to one of the creative professions given the evidence of his trendy haircut, the Rotring pen poking out from his shirt pocket and his Camper boots.

'Lucian Freud,' he announces.

'Yes.'

'I know one of his models.'

'Really?'

'Yes.'

Without invitation he flicks through the large book before his fat finger is planted firmly onto one of the glossy pages: 'Her,' he says. Inevitably it's one of Freud's nudes; one of his studies of women, arms and legs thrown wide, lying on his grubby sofa, and, given the light, probably in the afternoon. 'Apparently he was always trying to shag her.'

'I think he had a reputation for it.'

'Yeah. But she didn't let him.'

'Do you still know her?'

'Oh yeah,' the man says. 'Working on it.' He winks. I haven't seen anyone wink for a good few years. Like whistling, it's a dying art. Benny Hill springs to mind.

A brief diversion into the workroom to check the next shift. On the way I collect the 'Workroom Trolley' which is, as its name suggests, the trolley that goes back and forth to the workroom carrying stock to and from the main floors of the library. On the top of the trolley is a book, withdrawn by one of the morning staff. The note on it reads: 'Withdrawn. The book is damp and smells of stale cigarette smoke. Borrower messaged'. It's *Don't Die Young* by Alice Roberts.

The incidence of damaged books – accidentally or wilfully – is actually quite low. Perhaps people remember the punishment meted out to playwright Joe Orton and his partner Kenneth Halliwell. In 1962 the two of them were imprisoned for six months for stealing seventy-two books and 'wilfully' damaging others from the Hampstead and Islington libraries, including removing 1,653 plates from art books. Boredom, frustration and a shared delight in shocking the dreary establishment led them both to spend hours cutting up images, which they would then superimpose over the original book covers. When they were sentenced at Old Street Magistrates' Court, the *Mirror*'s headline was 'Gorilla in the roses'. This was a reference to the image of a monkey's head one of them had pasted in the centre of a rose on the cover of *Collins Guide to Roses*. The re-versioned image is strong and strangely affecting.

Orton also spent hours typing false blurbs onto the inside dust covers of novels. The yellow-jacketed Gollancz books were a favourite target because of their blank yellow inner flaps.

Halliwell, when interviewed by the police, said, 'I saw Orton typing on the covers of books. I read what he typed, and I considered it a criticism of what the books contained.'[22]

Underpinning this creative vandalism was Orton's anger and frustration – this is shared by a number of customers I've encountered. Orton rails at librarians in this interview he gave to the *Evening News* in 1967, but the blame belonged to the system:

> The thing that really put me in a rage about librarians was that I went to quite a big library in Islington and asked for Gibbon's *Decline and Fall of the Roman Empire*. They told me they hadn't got a copy of it. They could get it for me, but they hadn't one on their shelves . . . I was enraged that there were so many rubbishy novels and rubbishy books . . . libraries might as well not exist; they've got endless shelves of rubbish and hardly any space for good books.[23]

And that, in a nutshell, fifty years on, is still the heart of the libraries debate: is the borrower of *Fifty Shades of Grey* any less worthy of a membership card than the academic who yesterday wanted the two-volume Quentin Bell biography of Virginia Woolf fetching up from the store room? The literati signing the petition to save their local library have not, I bet, borrowed a book from any library since they were in their teens. It's not James Joyce but James Patterson (four books in the top-twenty most borrowed fiction titles 2014/15, according to Public Lending Right figures) who's keeping library stock churning. And when it comes to poetry it's not Shelley or Keats but a poetry collection that included this as an opener with an easy-going style and accessible imagery which is proving the most popular:

> O Botox, O Botox,
> I'm ever so keen,
> To look as I looked at the age of sixteen.

Pam Ayres' *You Made Me Late Again!* was the most borrowed poetry book of 2014/15.

And leading the nonfiction loans was, unsurprisingly, not Edward Gibbon, but Mary Berry. Have you heard of M. C. Beaton? I hadn't until I started working here. She's author of the *Agatha Raisin* and *Hamish Macbeth* crime-fiction books, and has been the most borrowed British author of books for adults for the last six years.

But, as is so often the case, it's not the lending of books that's currently taking up the time of the staff working in the library. Facilities Trev appears at the desk carrying a wallet. Being Trev, he waits for me to ask the question.

'Go on then. Whose is it?'

'Know what?'

'What?'

'Last week somebody hands in a wallet. Been found in the IT Suite. Open it. Five hundred and sixty euros in there. So I tannoy the name. Bloke comes and collects it. German. Never even thanks me. ... The last wallet that got handed in. This was a few days ago. Found in the public toilets on the first floor. I open it. Driving licence. A hundred and ninety quid in new notes. Probably not been in there long so I look at the photo and look for the bloke. I see him downstairs. Just sitting on one of the sofas, not reading or anything. I go up to him. I say,

"Are you missing anything, sir?" He looks up. Says "No." I say, "What about this?" and hand him his wallet. He thanks me. But he's upset, I can tell. He says, "I'm all at sixes and sevens." I ask him why. He says, "I've just buried my daughter. She was thirty-four. Three kids." I say, "I'm sorry," but there's nothing I can do for him.'

Relief is later provided in Children's when a young boy – about three – approaches the desk and asks if we have any books about diggers. I tell him I'm not sure but we can go and look. He follows willingly, his mother monitoring from a distance. On a low shelf we find a book about trucks with big wheels, which he is interested in.

'I like building sites, too,' he says. Together we find a book about cranes. His final request is for something on the Army. He'd spotted one as we hunted for the others. I add it to his collection and he takes them back to his mum, climbing onto her lap without permission and opening the book on cranes. The day seems better after that.

Carnegie

The results are finally out. The finance committee has pronounced. Those who have expressed an interest in taking
redundancy have all been granted their wish. Forty-two of the
workforce are leaving – a huge exodus of experience. Those
who are going are, by and large, doing so regretfully although
there are a couple who can't wait to get out of the place. The
senior staff are generally saddened by their departure; their
main concern is that they don't want to be around to see the
predicted decline in the service. There is no alternative. Budget
cuts of 30-odd per cent mean inevitable changes.

The effect on the service will be massive for some customers,
imperceptible to others. Those who continue to want to borrow
books might well find the queues at the service points longer.
Those, like the ninety-two-year-old woman who came in this
morning on another quest, will be obliged to fall back on their
own depleted resources. She was in no way remarkable. Just
another ninety-odd-year-old widow, alone now for just over a
year after losing her husband of some seventy years. She had
moved to the area, she explained, to live with her son in his flat.
He died young, shortly after her husband, leaving her entirely
alone in an alien city. Her main concern now is to find a GP's
surgery which will take her on as an NHS patient. She doesn't

know where to start. She has been walking for a couple of hours around the unfamiliar streets but has, so far, found only one private practice, who explained to her that to see a doctor would cost her £200. They failed to furnish her with the address of an NHS surgery within her catchment area. The present is a foreign country to her. She has no mobile phone, she does not use a computer. The agencies that once protected and defended her now persecute her. She is close to tears.

'I just don't know what to do,' she tells me. 'I know this isn't a library question, but could you help me find a GP?'

It's fairly quiet in Nonfiction today so I ask the woman to take a seat while I make some enquiries. It takes ten minutes to find a practice that will take her on. The receptionist I speak to on the phone promises to look after the woman when she comes in to register. I photocopy a map, circle the surgery in red and take it over to her where she waits, stiff-backed, taking no comfort from a seat she seems to feel she has no right to use. She seems overwhelmed, repeating that I have been very kind. I assure her it's part of the service – for now.

The actor Mark Rylance has now weighed in to the library debate calling libraries the 'fabric of our communities' as he joined in opposition to his local council's plans to close five out of ten of the borough's libraries and replace employees with volunteers. Rylance is quoted as saying the closures undermined the principle of education for all cherished by the likes of Scottish-American industrialist Andrew Carnegie, whose philanthropic legacy included 2,509 libraries worldwide such as the one in Herne Hill, which opened in 1906. 'To sell them off to private interests is a betrayal of the wishes of someone like Mr Carnegie who educated himself out of extreme poverty as an immigrant in America. How did he do that? At a library.'

Well, to some extent this is true. I know the name, of course, but I'm fairly ignorant about Andrew Carnegie so in a quiet moment I hunt out his name in the biographies section (Dewey: 920 CAR), and there I find a rare copy of his autobiography published by Constable in 1920 (interestingly, I note, the publishers of this book). Carnegie was the son of a Dunfermline handloom weaver whose family emigrated to Pennsylvania when independent cloth manufacturers were priced out of the market by the advent of steam machinery. Andrew Carnegie was thirteen when they left Scotland and crossed the Atlantic: 'New York was the first great hive of human industry among the inhabitants of which I had mingled, and the bustle and excitement of it overwhelmed me.'[24] From New York, the family took the Erie Canal by way of Buffalo and Lake Erie to Cleveland and then down the canal to Beaver – a journey of three weeks. From Beaver they took the steamboat up the Ohio to Pittsburgh.

Once established in Allegheny City, Carnegie's father realised hand-weaving was no longer a viable profession and took a job in a cotton factory. It was suggested to Carnegie's mother that Andrew could make a living peddling 'knicknacks' from a basket to the sailors on the river wharf. Carnegie's mother – a tough woman who'd worked hard to save the family from starvation back home – threw the man who had suggested it out of the house. Instead, Andrew was secured a job as a 'bobbin boy' in the factory where his father worked. From this, he progressed to messenger boy at the local telegraph office. He was an industrious and hard-working lad with a keen eye for the main chance. The hours were long, and he seldom got home before 11 p.m. 'This did not leave much time for self-improvement, nor did the wants of the family leave any money to spend on books.'[25]

Carnegie then heard of a local man – Colonel James Anderson – who had announced that he would open his library of over 400 books to 'working boys'. They were to be allowed to take out a single book each Saturday afternoon, which could then be exchanged for another on the following Saturday. This was a huge moment in Carnegie's life: 'Books which it would have been impossible for me to obtain elsewhere were, by his wise generosity, placed within my reach; and to him I owe a taste for literature which I would not exchange for all the millions that were ever amassed by man.'[26]

It was in tribute to the access he was given Colonel Anderson's library that, when Carnegie's massive fortune was made from steel, he donated millions of dollars to fund public libraries. As he wrote:

> It was from my own early experience that I decided there was no use to which money could be applied so productive of good to boys and girls who have good within them and ability and ambition to develop it, as the founding of a public library in a community which is willing to support it as a municipal institution.
>
> For if one boy in each library district, by having access to one of these libraries, is half as much benefited as I was by having access to Colonel Anderson's four hundred well-worn volumes, I shall consider they have not been established in vain.[27]

Carnegie's autobiography is hard to find nowadays, but there are a few copies in the library system. Nearly a hundred years old now, the arguments in it remain relevant.

But, as has been proved many times since I began working

here, this building, which just happens to house books for improvement and entertainment, is in greater demand as a sanctuary. It's warm. It has a roof, running water, toilets and, as such, when the nights are cold, it's a tough place to leave. As the tannoy announces that the library is now closed, one of the regulars, Sleepless Nigel, tells me he's had a bad day. I sympathise but remind him for the second time that the library has closed and he should leave. He's the only one left on the upper floor and is taking his time sorting out his rucksack, unplugging his laptop, putting his other belongings in a plastic bag. It's now five past seven and the library is otherwise devoid of customers – even the stragglers who tend to dash in just as the doors are being locked to use the toilets.

'Time to go.' I say again. I've radioed Facilities for support and they're on their way up.

'I've had a very stressful time,' Sleepless Nigel says. 'Don't hassle me.'

'I'm not hassling you. The library is closed. The doors will be locked.' Late leavers are particularly galling to staff members who are paid until closing time and no longer. Nigel has now had ten free minutes of my life.

Facilities Steph arrives and adds her voice to the suggestion that Nigel should leave.

'I need a piss,' Nigel pleads.

'No time. You'll have to go outside.'

'What – and piss in the street?'

Sleepless Nigel has been asleep for the past thirty minutes so his pleas that he hasn't had enough time to clear up are not met with sympathy.

'All right! All right! F*** you. I'll get out of your hair!' Finally, he makes it to the lift and leaves the building.

On the way home three street sleepers are fighting over ownership of the sheltered doorway of a vintage clothes shop. The pitch is popular not only because of the shelter, but also because it's on the corner of two small shopping streets thus doubling the number of potential begging targets. The regular who sleeps there guards it jealously. The other two suggest to him that he has no rights over it and it's their turn. They threaten to kick his head in. I don't wait for the outcome.

Bookmark 7

A shopping list (written on the back of a till receipt):

Bread,

Quinoa,

Oil,

Rice,

Cheese,

Bank,

Teeth

The Words We Use to
Say Goodbye

At the morning's staff briefing the manager announces that leaving cards are available to be signed in 'admin'. With the imminent exodus of forty-odd staff members there are a few dozen of them and the challenge will be to find something unique to say about each individual. A wake is planned at the library on the other side of the city on Friday night and contributions are to be placed in an envelope in the tearoom.

The table in the corner of the staffroom is laden with food each lunchtime. At Christmas and other seasons of celebration the library staff have a tradition of bringing in cakes and home-baked bread and savouries to be shared. This might well be the last week in which celebrations are conducted in this way – most of the organisers are leaving. To do what? I ask a few of them. All suggest they will have a few months to themselves before looking for some kind of voluntary work.

On *Breakfast Time* it was evident that the BBC has just woken up to the cuts. It was the third item on the eight o'clock news, the report suggesting that 8,000 jobs have 'disappeared' in six years. The spokeswoman for a new pressure group said she sees the rise of volunteer-run institutions as a bad thing: 'They often don't turn up to open the library when it's supposed to be open.

They don't have the training to do the things they need to do. Librarians adhere to a code of professional conduct in the same way that doctors, lawyers and accountants do. By bringing in thousands of volunteers, those ethics become watered down. Volunteers may harbour prejudices and biases and could prevent people from accessing information or using the library space. Council employees are held accountable for their conduct and librarians are accountable to their professional body – there is no such accountability for volunteers.'

Another pundit who holds an MA in librarianship is quoted as saying of the volunteer system, 'It atomises the public library system into various local clubs, run by people often without any training, who often do not have any long-term resources. 'Buoyed along by early optimism, such libraries may do well for a short few years, but what chance they have in the long term is anyone's guess.'

It's timely as those leaving the library here are serving out their final few days. The Buzzcocks' 'Everybody's Happy Nowadays' blares out ironically as the Van Boxes are processed. Today, there are two trolley shelves of saturated books – the result of torrential weekend rain caused by a hurricane and the fact that the lid to the Silver Bin was stuck open. Several gallons of water poured in, making a pulp of the returns.

But the place ticks over. The Travelling Man is in early, reporting continuing decline in his memory. He's had to come out of the house for a couple of hours because his cleaner is in. 'I can't just sit there watching people work,' he says. 'Just isn't me.' Today, he offers the story of his life as a props man for a television company. 'We had a laugh, a right laugh. We had to get the props from the stores for all the shows – dramas and whatnot, anything . . . anyway, we had this boss. Tall bloke,

Billy. Everybody hated him. Anyway, we had to bring up this coffin for a show so one of the fellows got in it and closed the lid. So we calls Billy over and says, "There's a problem with this coffin." Billy says, "What?" And my mate inside the coffin, he rattles the lid. Anyway, the studio is forty-foot long and Billy runs the whole length of it. Fast as he can. He gave us a right what for afterwards . . .'

The final stop on today's memory carousel sees the Travelling Man going back to his life post props – when he was a picture framer. Working with another man, they framed for some of the bigger West End galleries and worked with some of the leading artists of the 1960s, including Hockney.

'Anyway, one day we were delivering a van load of stuff to a gallery on Bond Street. Smart place. Gay guy was in charge. So we gets there with the van and the chap comes out to stand guard, in case anybody nicked anything. So he's standing there on the pavement and my mate goes up to him from behind, sticks his fingers in his back and says, "Don't move. We're taking the f***ing lot." The guy faints. Straight up. He faints, but the fellow I worked with he . . .'

I tune out. I'm sorry, but my mind has wandered. I see one of the old-timers talking to an old lady, another of the regulars. She's wishing him goodbye. It's his last day. She's short and thin and reaches up to hug him.

Back home I hear that the library-cuts story has been picked up by a number of news outlets. Jeremy Vine featured it on his lunchtime Radio 2 show, Nicky Campbell discussed it. The National Literacy Trust was quoted as saying:

Libraries play a crucial role in supporting early language development, giving children the opportunity to discover

new books and encouraging reading for enjoyment. They
also provide a space for adults to develop basic skills and
are social places for the whole community. Libraries are
vital for literacy across the UK and work most effectively
when library services are tailored to the needs of the local
community.

Dissenting voices suggest that libraries are now redundant in
the light of the internet, and one government spokesman denied
there had been a cut in the services. The *Guardian* reported that
libraries are facing the biggest crisis in their history.

The leaving party is tomorrow night.

A Literal Inconvenience

The party, given that it is held in a library, is a high-spirited one. Each departing member of staff is called to the front to receive their leaving card and riotous applause. Some dance, some anchor themselves beside the drinks table. It's a fitting occasion. Earlier in the day an email is circulated to all staff from one of the longer servers, which includes these lines: 'In an establishment that scaffolds free speech and free expression, it has been a rich and rewarding experience that not only benefitted me professionally but also personally ... However, ultimately, it has been the relationships with my friends and colleagues that will always be foremost in my thoughts.'

Only one member of staff fails to turn up for the early shift next day. His partner calls in to report that he's been throwing up all night and regrettably won't be able to make it in. Stevie Wonder accompanies the Van Box processing – loudly, until somebody turns it down. At the end of the morning briefing the duty manager asks: 'Anything else?'

A hand goes up – It's head of Facilities, Jo: 'Just to report on the new upstairs toilets.'

'OK.'

'So we've now opened the refurbished toilets and I was

hoping that I wouldn't have to put up any signage, but I think we might have to put up instructions.'

A nod.

'So the sinks don't have taps. There's an opening in the wall with a green light. You put your hands in there and the machine dispenses soap, then the light changes and it dispenses water. Then it changes again and it blow-dries your hands ... but people are having difficulty with it.'

It's agreed that signs might be a good idea on these counter-intuitive sink facilities.

One of the first customers of the day is an old-fashioned academic. Early twenties, he seems out of time. He's dressed in a nondescript sweater and jeans but would be better suited to more formal clothing, possibly Edwardian. He brings to mind a character in a Kafka novel. He is, in fact, Italian and is unerringly polite, addressing me at all times as 'sir'. He's in because he wants to borrow a book on population growth in the EU. It's obscure. There is only one copy on AbeBooks (the second-hand book internet site) but he's sure a library somewhere in the country will have it. I trudge off in search of the inter-library loans expert and find her in her lair at the corner of the main office. She has decades of expertise and knows how to deal with the politics of borrowing rare books from elsewhere in the country. We search for the book on her inter-library website and find eight copies. Two are in the British Library, but are reference-only copies so can't be loaned out. Three are the wrong edition (the polite gent is adamant he needs the 1990 edition, not the 1991 one). There are three further copies, two of which are in university libraries.

'No,' she says, 'neither of them will loan.'

Apparently some university libraries are parsimonious and will not let any books out. There is, though, a copy in a Glasgow library that will loan. The problem is that we have already got a book on loan from them and it's being returned late so Glasgow are not very happy with us. She will, however, approach them diplomatically and see what she can do. It's an eye-opener and rather dents the fond image I have of the universality of information and the underlying drive of all librarians to educate where they can.

I return to the polite gent and tell him that the inter-library loans expert is contacting Glasgow and she'll let him know the outcome. 'Thank you, sir, you've been most helpful.'

He leaves, disappearing into the mists of history to take his horse cab back to his dwelling house.

A male. early thirties, is also waiting for me by the desk. His Oakley sunglasses are parked on his tanned and shiny forehead, his head is shaved, he is wearing a tight white T-shirt and faded, arse-dropped denims. 'I just got told to f*** off by a young boy over there,' he says, pointing towards the study area.

'Ah.'

'I won't have it. I'm an adult and I won't have it. Will you ask him to leave, please?'

I collect the walkie-talkie and follow him into the long room, where thirty or forty people are studying silently.

'That's him, in the blue-and-grey striped T-shirt.'

Thirty or forty people stop studying and look up. We approach the four computers at the central carousel. At one of them is the youth he's identified: a lean South American boy with designer stubble. He looks up reluctantly from the screen with a degree of weariness.

Oakley man says, 'He swore at me. I don't like being told to f*** off. And him . . .' He gestures towards the white-haired, middle-aged man sitting next to the boy. 'He was typing very loudly. Disturbing everyone.'

The attention of the room is now on the exchange.

'I didn't tell you to f*** off,' the boy says.

A woman behind me chips in: 'He's the troublemaker.' She's pointing the finger at the pumped complainer.

'That's right,' the white-haired man says. 'He was swearing at the boy.'

Other voices are raised in support of the student.

'So this is what this is!' Mr Oakley says, drawing himself up to his full height. 'A heterosexual conspiracy!' he levels the charge at the room in general.

There's an awkward silence. Everybody hates him.

'Let me book you onto another computer,' I offer. The man declines and says he might come back later. He flounces off.

Because I'm upstairs in Nonfiction I use the opportunity to check out the new toilets. I discover two washbasin-type devices in white porcelain sunk into the wall – two huge white open mouths. A soft green glow radiates down from somewhere inside them, bathing the interior of the mouth in light. I stick in my right hand with a degree of wariness and a glob of white liquid issues onto my palm. A brief pause and then warm water cascades down. Again a pause and then the interior hand-dryer fires up and dries my hand. Impressive. One of the two new toilet cubicles has an A4-sized piece of paper taped to the door alerting potential users to the fact that the toilet is 'Out of Order' followed by 'sorry for the inconvenience'. I don't think this is ironic. In the other cubicle there are two empty cans of Stella Artois on the floor, nestling against the pan. I remove the cans and take them back to my workstation. A woman, studying at one of the desks, watches me drop them in the bin and doubtless marks me down as a serious drinker.

Mugs

The lugubrious American singer songwriter J. J. Cale is entertaining the staff today as the Van Boxes are processed. I say good morning to one of the few remaining managers. She stayed late to clear up after the party and reports that there were five crates of empty bottles. Not bad going for a profession perceived to be staffed by embittered spinsters in dusty clothes whose sole contribution to the atmosphere is going around shushing people. The stock sitcom caricature no longer holds (evidence that those writing sitcoms haven't recently used the service) and hasn't held for decades. Almost everybody here has another life. It's the preserve of poets, artists, sculptors, writers, subsidising their other lives by working between the stacks. They all bring something to the place. But today, in the aftermath of the mass exodus, two of the tables in the tearoom bear orphaned mugs. These are those left behind by the departed. The staff cupboard has been cleared and these orphans are awaiting adoption. If they aren't, a scrawled sign says, they will be disposed of. I count 104 mugs on the table.

Those who remain, now that their friends and colleagues have left, are shell-shocked. 'Today "x" would have been in' is the repeated refrain, a reminder that the mood of a workplace is dictated more by the people there than the work in which they're employed, with some obvious exceptions – hangman, for example.

The mood of the customers is similarly muted, or perhaps it's transference. The Nonfiction floor is full of students studying, a number of them trailing their laptop leads dangerously across access routes. When spotted by the staff, we invite them to remove these trip hazards. Most comply with guarded hostility. The young generation is not used to being censured in any way. 'But my laptop is just about to run out,' one girl responds angrily.

'I'm sorry, but the cable is across the main walkway, somebody will trip.'

'Well, what am I supposed to do?' Her anger ratchets up a notch.

What to suggest?

Two young students, new lovers by the look of their body language, are sitting close to each other, sharing oxygen. Their papers are strewn across the table, as are their laptops. But the laptops are shut and each of them is leaning an elbow on the table, their head resting on their hand. Their faces are close, they are speaking quietly and intimately, but they become audible to the rest of the table as an argument breaks out.

I catch a word: ' . . . funny,' the girl says.

The boy retains his smile. He says, 'I do.'

'You don't.'

Louder now. 'I do.'

'Give me an example.'

He thinks, but can't come up with one.

'You just don't think I'm funny.'

'You are funny.'

'I know you don't. When I tell you something funny, you don't laugh.'

'I do!' He makes the mistake of smiling, tries to reach out a finger towards her hand, presumably to stroke it. Too late. She stands, collects her papers and laptop and storms out. He waits. His smile is extinguished. Slowly he collects his own belongings and follows her out.

Later, I see them on the piazza. It's raining lightly but they're sitting on one of the benches in their damp denims; he has his arm around her shoulder. She's leaning against him smoking a cigarette – a roll-up. Hostilities are over for a while.

A couple of the regulars are in today. Spencer enters with his jaunty walk and heads for his usual seat in the Fiction section. Joseph is trailing round after his daughter, who is wearing a long, diaphanous ballet skirt over her other clothing. He is smiling, filming her on his mobile phone. As the day progresses he continues to follow her around, walking several miles.

And then, towards the end of the day, the Thin Man comes in: Mr Jones. His ban still holds in a couple of libraries, but not this one. He clocks me; I clock him. He holds my gaze for a moment and then installs himself on one of the PCs, where he remains for an hour. When his time runs out he approaches the service point at which one of the young female library officers is working. She doesn't know Mr Jones. Doesn't know his modus operandi. Just a polite, well-dressed, well-turned out man who's expressing an interest in her, being friendly. I remember this. It comes flooding back. Most customers would, when their enquiry had been answered, move off, but Mr Jones doesn't. At least he does, but he circles one of the pillars and approaches the young woman from another direction and stands now on her left-hand side. She is still smiling, but she doesn't know Mr Jones. I hope he's not fishing – a casual, 'Where do you live?' . . .

I call Facilities and Facilities Steph responds and comes to find me. I explain my concern. I'm not suggesting Mr Jones is doing anything wrong. I'm just saying . . .

'Yeah,' Steph says. 'I know.'

She watches him until he leaves. This is not an isolated library on the outskirts of the city – where, during the winter, the staff leave in darkness for the bus home. Soon these libraries will be single-staffed. Often there are only one or two customers in the library during the last hour of opening. In the past it has been Mr Jones, waiting, disappearing, then there at the bus stop, waiting.

Bad Juju

No question that the city has its moods and today is a bad juju day. Too many people are bad tempered. If it was just me, then I wouldn't forward this as a suggestion. But it's not. The conversation in the tearoom is all about rude, intolerant customers throwing their weight and, occasionally, their books around. A normally mild-mannered colleague admits that she has wanted to slap every other customer. This is compounded by the computer system seizing up mid-morning, making issuing tricky and anything more complicated impossible. Not our fault, but the staff take the blame for the ever-failing system. It's the closest I have ever got to calling a customer a f***stick, kicking over the terminal and storming out. When a full concession customer (two free hours on the computer ostensibly to aid job seeking) tells me YouTube is inaudible, I resist suggesting he get on with his job searching and stop watching Beyoncé videos, which he seems to do most days, sitting a little too close to the screen.

When he has gone I wonder, in this age of heightened racial awareness, whether 'bad juju' is in some way an offensive term to some, as yet unidentified, minority group. I check it out. The Online Slang dictionary suggests that it's an action likely to be harmful in a Karmic way – so maybe to identify a day as a bad juju day is not appropriate – but today certainly feels that way.

Customer hostility is common the world over. Don Borchert's *Library Confidential* reports his dealings with those categorised as 'MMM' on their cards. MMM indicates the customer is trouble – 'guard your privates, you're in for a rough ride'. Borchert's response to these people is clever. He doesn't give in to his instinct to call them a f***stick or wrestle them to the ground. He lets them kick off and then he goads them. This pushes them so hard that their usual low-key, sotto voce attack on the isolated staff member becomes public, Security can be called and the customer expelled. He tried it with a regular MMM, who demanded that Borchert put his books into a bag. Having put up with the man's unreasonable behaviour and rudeness for several minutes, Borchert informs him that 'The transaction is over.' This pushes the man's button so hard, he's finally led out by Security, threatening Borchert with physical violence next time he comes in.

The violence perpetrated by the customers here tends to be more malevolent – evil, low-key, whispered. A lamented colleague who left in the recent exodus wouldn't take it. He gave as good as he got, without pause – and if the customer tried to up the ante his next response would be 'Right! Please wait there, sir [or madam]. I will go and fetch a complaints form, which you are more than welcome to fill in.' Having marched off, he'd go to the tearoom for a few minutes to calm down, and then return with the form (which he would always have about his person). Inevitably the irate troublemaker would already have lost patience and left.

Against this hostile backdrop, Moneysavingexpert.com has just published the results of a survey asking 'Will you miss your local library if it is shut down?' OK, quite a loaded question, but of over 200,000 replies, 195,238 said they would; 55 per cent of the respondents were under fifty-five.

'Den of Geek' (the website set up by the publisher Felix Dennis) has now weighed in, posting:

> Once you adopt the town library as your refuge, you're paired for life. The relationship you start with that municipal brick building will outlast every other. Boyfriends, girlfriends, best friends and spouses will drift in and drift out, but the sense of inner calm you derive from functional shelving and plastic-coated paperbacks never leaves. You're a library dweller, a literal card-carrying member.[28]

I pass Trev on my way upstairs and catch the end of a sentence: '. . . standing in six inches of s**t.' He's reliving the events of a few months ago when the sewer backed up and he spent much of Saturday night carrying buckets of human waste across the piazza to empty into a nearby drain; '. . . twenty buckets.' I think the full shock of it is just hitting home. Perhaps he has PTSD. 'Amazing what people put down there,' he goes on. 'Hand towels. That's stupid. They just swell up. And jumpers. Jumpers! How do you get a jumper down a toilet?'

He goes on to explain that the sewer situation will never be resolved unless they dig up the piazza and re-lay the sewer pipes. 'They sent the cameras down,' he says. 'Rats. They were coming up to the camera and looking in . . . Anyway, they send a wheel down there every three months to grind down the join between the pipes, get rid of the limescale. Hey-ho . . .'

Today's strange day closes with a female customer, manic, dashing up and down the fashion bookstack. We are closed but she won't leave. 'I need a book! I need a book on fashion. I'm going to stay with my mother and it will be intolerable without a book. Intolerable!' She's burning very bright, almost totally out of control. She lists a few fashion icons: Galliano, Gaultier, Chanel, Sander. Finally, she spots one, grabs it from the shelf and dashes for the lift.

The library is now clear. The day's weirdness retreats with the customers and all that's left is silence and peace as the books begin to reassert their benevolent hold on the place.

Going to Bed with
Henry Miller

The music of pint-sized crooner Prince is today's soundtrack to the early morning labours. He died yesterday – another shock pop death. News emerges from the American press that he helped preserve a little bit of Louisville history. In 2001 the musician donated $12,000 to support the Western Branch Library, which over the years had faced threats of closure. He asked that the award be kept private.

When the doors open at ten, I count forty-three people surging in, the students literally running up the stairs – and eight pushchairs. It's coming up to exam time and by eleven all of the desks upstairs are occupied by students. More than 100 of them. None of these will show in the figures for library attendance as none of them are taking out books. Add to that the two circles of them sitting on the floor of Fiction and there are over 130 young people in here today, as there have been over the past two weeks and which there will continue to be until the exam period is over. How to quantify them on the spreadsheets?

But there's a downside to this. Today, one of the early customers is one of the regulars. A woman, mid/late eighties, who arrives each week with a closely, neatly written list of the books in black biro she asks one of the staff to find for her. Her eyesight is poor; she's awaiting laser surgery. She's looking for the new Harlan Coben and one by Sophie Hannah. I find the Hannah for her in large print. She reads the back and realises she's already had it out. While I go in search of her next choice, *If She Did It* by Jessica Treadway – a well-reviewed new thriller – she sets off on her own hunt. We arrive back at the desk at the same time. The Treadway is in, and she's found a new copy on the classics promotion: Henry Miller's *The Rosy Crucifixion*.

'Have you read Henry Miller?' I ask her.

'No.'

'He's quite . . . racy.'

'I'm not sure what that means.'

'I mean he is a brilliant writer, but he's . . .'

The woman is looking at the text now. She pauses. Squints harder. 'Oh,' she says. 'I see. That's fine. I'll read it in bed.'

While I issue the books she mentions that she has to find a book for her husband. He's a little older than she is and he finds it hard to get out.

'He used to come in here all the time,' she tells me. 'But last year he broke his back.'

I express sympathy.

'Yes, he got up in the night to use the loo. Next thing, I heard a huge crash. I got out of bed and found him at the bottom of the stairs . . . I called an ambulance. This was midnight. By seven the next morning he was still in the ambulance outside the hospital waiting for a bed. It was chaos. Anyway, he was in there for a couple of days. They scanned him and said he was all right. Three days later we got a call just after we went to bed. It was the hospital. They said they'd reviewed the scans and he'd broken his back. They were sending an ambulance and he shouldn't move. He was in there for weeks. But they looked after him. Luckily it was just his back and not his neck. But he's quite jittery now . . .'

'I'm sorry.'

'Yes. So he managed to come in last week and went upstairs here. He loves the library. But upstairs was full of students at the desks. There wasn't a single chair – and he needed to sit down . . . he went to one of the tables and asked if somebody would mind standing up so he could rest – and they just laughed at him.'

I make a lame apology – explain these are the library users of the future. They're not in to use the books, but to use the place as a study hall. We have to encourage them otherwise places like this have no future. I add that I've found the students to be generally polite and well behaved (knowing in my heart that they are generally not). But I assure her that should this happen again her husband must ask one of the staff members for a seat and one will be found. She thanks me, but seems unconvinced as she takes her Henry Miller home to read in bed.

I encounter Trev on the way upstairs to Nonfiction and ask how it's going. 'Reports of a man in a checked, short-sleeved shirt worrying kiddies,' he says sombrely.

'Very amusing.' Today, I'm the only one in the library wearing a checked, short-sleeved shirt.

'A few of the usuals in upstairs. Keeping an eye on them. Unfortunately, they're behaving themselves.'

Perhaps to tilt the balance in favour of the student users of the place, a young female student (A-level age) who's working at a table with a friend returns from the Ladies clutching something she's found on the floor between the Nonfiction shelves. I hear her ask her friend if she's dropped a £10 note. The girl replies that she hasn't. I assume that will be the end of the conversation and the two girls will happily use the proceeds for their lunch. The girl then approaches the desk, hands over the £10 note explaining that she found it, it's not hers and she wants to hand it in. I thank her and feel I should commend her honesty but know that that would devalue the transaction. The girl returns to her table. I radio Facilities, explaining the find, and Facilities Steph arrives to collect the money and put it in the safe. Later, when I return from lunch, Facilities Steph comes to find me. 'I want to offer you a head's up.'

'Yes?' I sense I'm in for a telling off.

'When you're radioing about lost property, don't give the details over the walkie-talkie.'

'OK.'

'Only somebody claimed the £10 – a young man. But there was something not quite right about it. Know what I'm saying?' She raises an eyebrow.

'It wasn't his? He overheard me calling you?'

'Maybe.'

For weeks there has been no sign of the phantom cyclist. But, that night, as I'm walking past the library on the way into town with my wife, from a distance we hear the tinny sound of music. The cyclist emerges from a side street. He is travelling, as usual, at great speed. His cycle has now got a wicker basket attached to the handlebars and inside the basket is a small speaker from which 1930s dance-band music is emanating. The man is wearing plastic flowers in an Alice band. He circles the piazza twice, and then heads off up the road.

Last Words

The day after a bank holiday usually means the network computer system starts playing up. The theory is that because all of the participating libraries in the conglomerate log in at the same time and dump their records, the system can't cope with the volume and freezes up entirely or runs slow (those who administer the system deny this is an issue). So it is this morning, with queues of irritated customers waiting at each service point demanding to know why we're keeping them waiting. Today, as is increasingly the case, the systems failures are regarded as the fault of those at the service points. When a system is under pressure it's those on the frontline that bear the blame. These are also, by definition, the ones doing their best to keep the ship from sinking. From what I know of the NHS through acquaintances, the same applies.

A rare moment of sympathy from a hangdog man returning four large books on model railways. I explain the circumstances; beg his patience. Wearily, he responds that he also works for the council and he's used to bearing the brunt of the blame.

The patience of everybody is wearing thin, and this is not improved when a feisty old woman peels away from the knitting group, stands by the lectern and angrily asks if there's a discussion group she can join.

'A knitting discussion group?' I ask. It seems like a reasonable question.

'No. Politics. Anything. A DISCUSSION GROUP.'

I explain to her that there are a number of book groups, both private and library run, as well as a number of informal groups that meet in the library but there are not any formal discussion groups.

She's now irate. Jabbing a finger towards my face she says: 'You want to get your finger out!'

'Do I?'

'Yes. If you want to survive.'

She stalks back to her chums, knitting and chatting at the low tables by Periodicals. She says something to the group and they look disapprovingly in my direction. Later in the day I learn that she has had the same conversation with three of my colleagues, all of whom have explained to her that the discussion groups held in the community libraries are all organised by private individuals and she is more than welcome to organise one herself.

Beyond the aggression, the woman, perhaps, has a point. Such initiatives fall to those who manage the place, who provide strategies for preserving the services in the face of the onslaught of cuts. Unfortunately, most of those people have now also been cut. The manager on duty tonight between five and seven has never managed a library team. If the computers fail then she will not have a clue how to resolve the issue. The staff will have to bear the brunt. Eventually it will become intolerable.

Libraries across the world are approaching this re-versioning with different strategies; the tendency of many is to move away from the core business of book-lending and towards multi-purpose community centres. The problem with this is that the further they move away, the more vulnerable they are. Why not just have a blank community space in the centre of a city, staff it with a couple of volunteers and allow it to be booked by anyone who wants it? But if it's a bookable space then why not sell it off and raise some short-term money?

The effect of the 'cuts' will be felt like this. Not immediately, but in hundreds of small ways, a slow build-up of irritation. Outbursts, staff sickness due to stress. There are only so many times you can take being shouted at for something that is not your fault – and which, in most cases, you work hard to preserve.

An elderly woman, quite deaf, comes to the counter and asks me to issue her two Large Print books.

'Oh,' she says, as I attend to them. 'Can you do something else for me?'

'Of course.'

'Well, my husband died three weeks ago and I keep getting my library ticket mixed up with his.'

The woman is warding off tears. I explain that I can cancel his account. She says she would appreciate it.

When she leaves I find her husband's account. He was born in 1933. His name was Michael. I press the cross at the top of the screen and the system asks me to confirm that I want to 'resign' the customer. I press 'OK' and Michael's life is eradicated.

On another occasion I hear of a ninety-nine-year-old man: 'a good man'. His neighbour tells me this when she brings in his books. They are all overdue by a couple of weeks but she says she hasn't had time to return them. She apologises. She says she's been busy arranging his funeral. She doesn't mention her neighbour's name but she says she is sad that he didn't make his hundredth birthday. He had no family and she is reticent about doing anything about his flat but she cleaned it up as best she could and washed his sheets. She says she wanted to leave the flat clean and tidy for whoever went in there.

He was a tough old man. He didn't talk about his life but preferred to live in the present, which she tries to do herself. She also lives alone and, despite the age difference, felt very close to her neighbour. She shows me a photograph of him. He is smiling – an impish smile – and he is sitting in his wheelchair in front of a pub bar. A glass charity jar of coins is behind him on the counter. He is wearing a smart tweed jacket, a tie, a white shirt. His neighbour is standing behind him, her hand on his shoulder.

She tells me she thinks he was in the Army – not just National Service, but he perhaps stayed on. She thinks he might have been in intelligence. She says she is drawn to his belongings – to the cupboards and drawers but she doesn't feel she has the right so she will leave them to whoever clears out the flat. She organised the funeral and she was the only mourner.

The books she returns – the last books he read were – *East of Eden* by John Steinbeck, *Vintage Williams* – a collection of the short stories of Tennessee Williams – and, for light relief, *The Adventure of the Christmas Pudding* by Agatha Christie. He died in hospital of pneumonia but his neighbour said he was well cared for and she was glad. There is a bookmark in *Vintage Williams*. I open the book to the marked page. He has put the book aside at the end of a story. Before he slept his final sleep, perhaps the last words he read were these, the closing of the story 'The Malediction':

Only a single instant she struggled against him: clawed his shoulder and arm in a moment of doubt. *My God, My God, why hast Thou forsaken me?* Then the ecstasy passed and her faith returned, they went away with the river. Away from the town, away and away from the town, as the smoke, the wind took from the chimneys – Completely away.[29]

Brexit Boolsheet

The tannoy bing-bongs at 9.55 just after the staff have dispersed from the daily briefing and are on their way to the work stations. It's the duty manager: 'Please be aware that a bird is inside the building. No need to radio. Facilities are aware but we're hoping it will go out the way it came in. Thank you.'

A radio crackles and we hear: 'What kind of bird is it?'

'A bird. There's only one.'

'OK.'

It's two days after the EU referendum and many of the customers are visibly and vocally shocked. The first to express concern is a woman who looks like she's seen a road accident.

'I just can't believe it,' she says. 'I've never been so shocked. I need something to read so I won't have to think about it.'

Three newish crime novels are her chosen remedy.

The writer Bella Bathurst's contribution to *The Library Book* suggests that what people choose to read *in extremis* is often surprising:

Within the first six months of the Second World War, library issues across Britain had risen by 20 per cent, and in some areas by 50 per cent. Evacuees and women whose sons or husbands were away fighting – people, in other words, who had the strongest need to see the world otherwise – were among the keenest users. In London, some authorities established small libraries in air-raid shelters. The unused Tube Station at Bethnal Green had a library of 4000 volumes and a nightly clientele of 6000 people.[30]

The next customer is equally distraught, also for Brexit-related reasons. 'Ooh dear. Ooh, dear,' she begins. She's perhaps in her mid/late seventies, desiccated skin, a violet gilet under her mac, blonde, thin hair, her own teeth (predominantly black). She is fierce, angry and determined.

'They've arrived already,' she announces.

'Who?'

'Outside, on the lawn. Hundreds of them: refugees.'

I peer over her shoulder to see two African women with backpacks settling themselves onto the AstroTurf. The sun has just come out after a period of heavy rain.

'They're not bloody refugees. They're criminals,' the woman explains. 'Now we're supposed to be able to get rid of them. But we won't because they'll all bloody come in before we can get out of Europe. That's what'll happen.'

She asks me to issue her a Peter James book. 'I used to use the big machines, but I can't now.' She points towards the automatic returns/issues RFIDs.

I hand back the book.

'There's nowhere to talk to anybody nowadays,' she says, 'to have a coffee and chat.'

I suggest she could have a coffee and chat in the coffee shop here. 'Nooo,' she says. 'It's full of fat old men. All they want is young women. I went up to a drop-in centre last week. Alzheimer's and such. I said I wanted to talk – you know – come

in for a chat. They wanted £10. I said, "What for?" "Transport,"
they said. I said I'd come here on my own two feet. They said
it was for the lunch, I said I didn't want bloody lunch, I just
wanted to chat.'

I smile and wait for her to reach some kind of conclusion.

'I travel a lot. I've done it rich and poor. I used to go to
Tenerife but they started bombing it. Stayed there in the winter.
They used to put the heating on first thing. You'd wake up to
snow on the ground but it would be warm. Then they'd turn it
off. You'd go to the reception and ask why they'd turned the
heating off. They'd say it was because everybody went out. I
said they hadn't gone bloody out because it was snowing and
they were all old and all they wanted was to keep warm. Yes,
I've travelled – backpacked and five-star. I've seen the world
from both sides. I can't settle, you see.'

'But you're settled in this city now?'

'God no! NO! What I do is get a single ticket. Go somewhere.
Move on. I'm not staying here. No bloody way. But I'd like a
chat. I mean in those five-star hotels you could talk to men but
they were gigolos. Gigolos. Spanish mainly. They just wanted
your money. I had money then. Not now. Not bloody now.'

And with that, she leaves, pausing to make one more muttered
comment about the refugees on the AstroTurf.

A final, mid-afternoon contribution to the Brexit debate
comes from a young hyperactive lad who has come in with
three friends, presumably on their way home from school. The
lad is holding court, bouncing up and down on the balls of
his feet. 'Yeah, well, it's all boolsheet, this Europe thing, see?
They say they're gonna have to close all Nando's but they're
not, it's boolsheet.'

Goodbye, Alexandria

Today, there's a severe staff shortage. Five library officers have called in sick and, instead of the usual twenty or so people attending the morning briefing, there are only ten. The duty manager looks around and announces that it's going to be a difficult day. It's half-term and she's never managed the library with so few staff. With the departure of forty-odd staff members this moment was inevitable. We have to stand our ground – customers will 'just have to wait' instead of being served immediately. The old-timers exchange glances. This is all very well in theory; in practice this will mean frayed tempers on both sides of the counter.

It's rare for a fight to break out so soon after the doors open but today it's barely two minutes after opening that, from the vantage point of the main desk, I hear voices being raised in the Young People's area behind me. This is a room off the main floor that houses the teenage fiction and nonfiction stock, several low hoppers of graphic novels, some comfy low sofas, the more populist mags (gamer's magazines, *Empire* and *Heat*), a number of PCs lined against a wall and four small circular tables for study with three chairs drawn up to each one. Although there is no sign advertising the fact, this is not an area for adults to lurk and ogle the young people or for the street sleepers to catch half an hour or so of sleep. Because of the lack of such signage, a couple of dodgy characters and various street sleepers regularly push their luck and skulk in there until they are asked to leave. This usually provokes mock incredulity and an argument on the grounds that were adults not allowed to use this space then this information should be advertised – which undoubtedly it should (and, incidentally, now is).

The exception to the 'no adults' policy are tutors. There are a number of these who come in regularly to work with mainly school-excluded children. These children habitually sit with their patient freelance teachers, goading them, eating crisps, telling them they are tired/bored or angry and trying any strategy to divert them from the task at hand, which is, presumably, an attempt to load some information into their damaged and partially closed minds. These children are not, from what I've observed, unintelligent – they can easily get the better of their tutors, but they employ their intelligence largely to undermine the process being used to increase it. The tutors, the majority of them private, tolerate this behaviour. They'll be paid whatever the outcome of the session and because expectations for their pupils are undoubtedly minimal, they have no vested interest in exceeding them. If anything, the opposite is the case. So long as their charges remain excluded then the tutors will have the pleasure of their company and the income this generates for years to come.

I leave the desk regretfully, having settled myself for an hour of relatively sedentary inactivity, to find a short-sleeved (but tie-wearing), balding, middle-aged man angrily stuffing some papers back in to his ancient briefcase and telling one of the regulars (when I see who it is my heart sinks) that he is 'a very rude man'.

'No, you're rude,' the regular says.

'No. You are!'

'You are.'

I watch, enjoying the playground spectacle of two late middle-aged men shouting at each other, but then the man with the briefcase spots me and I have no choice but to enter the ring.

'Can I help?'

'Yes, you can,' briefcase man says. 'I arrived at this table immediately after you opened and sat down to wait for my pupil, when this gentleman came and plonked himself down at the table. I explained the circumstances to him but he refuses to move.'

I turn to the regular. He's a troublesome man. Unlikeable, belligerent, but not criminal or dangerous. He knows his rights and exercises them on a daily basis.

'I can sit anywhere I like,' he says.

The table is a small one with just enough room for two full-sized people to sit together in comfort.

'But I explained I was waiting for my pupil,' Briefcase says.

'I don't care,' Regular says. 'This is a library, not a school.'

'I'm afraid this area is for young adults,' I explain to him. I know he knows this because we've had this discussion before.

He turns his fire back towards Briefcase. 'He's conducting a commercial operation from here,' he says. 'I have as much right to sit here as he does. Probably more.' This is a shrewd line of attack as most of the tutors are private and use the library's facilities for free. It's a murky area. But he's picked the wrong tutor this time.

'I'm a schoolteacher,' Briefcase tells him. 'I am, as I said, meeting a pupil from my school here.' He concludes with this, to me: 'But this rude man wants the table so he can have it.'

'You're the rude man,' Regular says. I'm hoping Briefcase will continue the 'you are' argument but he doesn't. He surveys the small area, looking for another table to use. Unfortunately, during the altercation, the other tables have become occupied by students.

'I'm sorry,' I say to Regular, 'there are tables in the main area and you're welcome to sit there but, as I said, this is the Young People's area.'

'I've had this out with the council five times. Five times!' He holds up his right hand, palm towards me and spreads his fingers in a visual representation of the number five. 'I want to see a manager.'

'OK,' I say. 'I'll call one.'

I summon one of the two duty managers by walkie-talkie. He arrives. I précis the circumstances with admirable (I think) clarity, taking care to remain as neutral as possible, and leave him to moderate.

I encounter another angry man later in the day in Nonfiction. He is sitting at one of the drop-in computers and hurling abuse towards the screen. He jabs a finger and swears. His brow is drawn back tight. He is almost speechless with anger but he's silently mouthing: 'F*** you! F*** YOU!' It's a full-on road-rage incident and I wonder who he's swearing at. Wandering from the desk and standing at his shoulder, I'm surprised to see there's actually nothing on the screen except for the log-on page.

Today, the library provides a venue for a number of activities. There's a festival going on in the city and a number of the conference rooms and side rooms have been booked for events. Two rooms on the mezzanine are being used for creative writing. In the foyer, adults and children are scribbling images onto A4 sheets of paper to illustrate the 'City Reads' promotion (an annual event designed to encourage as many people as possible to read the same book and engage with each other having done so). Electronic noises are emanating from the community space where children seem to be engaged in something involving cardboard, pens and sticky tape. Outside a tent has been erected on the piazza for a temporary music venue and the street has been closed off, enabling a young band to set up and entertain the passers-by with their peculiar hillbilly music. One of the women working on the book promotion passes and tells me that they've been amazed at the numbers coming in. 'It's the third place,' she explains.

'The what?'

'The third place.' She wanders off.

There's perhaps a lesson here for those who want to save this institution. At the main desk today, in two hours, I issue perhaps ten books but I am busy booking people onto computers, joining people (mainly to use the computers), telling people which room they can find the creative writing group, the LGBT photography event, the 'City Reads' event. Only one customer asks me to look up a book for him (*The Days of Abandonment* by Elena Ferrante). Customers are, of course, in and books are being issued and returned via the automatic machines, but the primary function of this place today is a community hub – an old-fashioned village green with plate-glass windows.

'The third place', I later discover, is a term coined by urban sociologist Ray Oldenburg. He identifies them as the public places on neutral ground where people can gather and interact. In contrast to first places (home) and second places (work), third places allow people to put aside their concerns and simply enjoy the company and conversation around them. They, 'host the regular, voluntary, informal, and happily anticipated gatherings of individuals beyond the realms of home and work'.[31] The main streets, post offices, cafés and libraries are the heart of a community's social vitality. They not only promote social equality (who knows or cares what somebody owns or earns in these places?), they provide a setting for grassroots politics.

It's an interesting concept. There's no doubt that the habit of public association is being lost and, with it, the places where we can find companionship and psychological support. Post offices, local pubs, libraries and even high streets are disappearing. When all of the third places are gone, then we'll all be forced to live in the fourth place – the bleak, isolated world viewed through the screen of a personal computer.

Two young lads were on local TV last night. They were reporters for a children's newspaper celebrating its tenth anniversary. To mark the occasion, they'd been invited to talk to David Cameron. The anchorman invited the first lad to share what he'd asked the Prime Minister. The boy had asked Cameron about why he was closing libraries – or reducing their hours.

'And what did the PM say?' the anchorman asked.

The lad reported that Cameron said that technology meant we no longer needed libraries. What he should perhaps have said was that technology means that his children and the children of his west London chums don't need libraries.

Last night, I dipped once again into *The Library Book* and read the essay by Tom Holland. His contribution examines the role of libraries in passing down information from generation to generation and concludes that we shouldn't overstate their importance. He writes: 'for all the immeasurable debt of gratitude we owe the librarians of Alexandria, it is as well to remember that the physical transmission of manuscripts from classical antiquity into the Middle Ages and the Renaissance owed nothing to libraries founded by any emperor or king. What has come down to us today derived instead from altogether more marginal institutions: the equivalent of run-down libraries, perhaps, in a financially-squeezed inner city borough. Pages stuffed into a vase; papyrus scraps buried beneath the crumbling of provincial walls; musty folios stored in a monastery's vaults: these are what survived the obliteration of the ancient world's imperial collections of books.'[32]

The debate goes on, and will continue to go on, but if the most senior member of the government at the time of writing considers libraries solely as places where information is provided then the battle is lost.

Reading Allowed

Those who have expressed an interest in leaving have now gone. Those who want to remain have been invited to reapply for their own jobs. The deadline is next week. Casuals are filling the gap but their days, too, are numbered. The higher grade staff applying for high-grade posts have now been interviewed and been phoned to be given the good news – or called in to the office to be told they were unsuccessful.

The library operates, just, throughout the morning. The queues are long, people are fractious, and some of the routine things that should have been done are forgotten. One of them is the putting out of the sign for the afternoon reading group. They meet every Friday at 2 p.m. in one of the side rooms and a table is reserved for them. For a couple of hours, they take it in turns to read a book out loud, and then discuss it. The staff member with responsibility for putting out the reservation sign is among the sick and nobody has remembered to do it. As a result, just before two, three women approach the front desk and ask why the table has not been reserved for them. The women are all Asian.

I radio the duty manager and explain the situation and she tells me that it's down to me to go into the side room and turf out the seven people sitting in there, explaining the levels of sickness in the library and suggesting they go elsewhere. There is not a single chair available anywhere in the place, so where that might be is unclear. She suggests that the sign for the group is in the book-group cupboard. I should arm myself with it and 'man up'. The sign is not in the book-group cupboard. Among the chaos of signage under the main desk, however, I find one labelled 'Reserved for Asian Women's Reading Group – 2 p.m.'. This seems the most likely candidate so I return to the desk to explain to the women that I've found the sign and am going to try and secure their space for them.

'What's that?' one of the women asks.

'Your sign.'

'No, it's not.'

'No?'

'No, we're the Reading Aloud group.'

'Ah.' Awkward. By now they have been joined by three others – all Caucasian. I have made an inadvisable racial assumption.

Thankfully, those at the table in the side room leave without any fuss and the Reading Aloud group gather – along with a new member: a slightly odd, very chippy and disinhibited woman who dominates the proceedings from the moment she sits down. I leave them to it and return to the desk, only to be summoned five minutes later by one of the Asian women who explains that the interloper is being difficult. She is complaining that one of the members of the group smells. More precisely that her feet smell, and she's not happy. Thankfully, I have a tea break and hand the problem over to my colleague who has just come on shift and is less stressed.

I've seen most of the regulars over the past couple of weeks. Last Wednesday *Sons of Anarchy* Alan arrived at the desk with Season 4. I issued it to him. He thanked me. I asked if he'd had his tattoos done yet. 'Next week,' he said. 'My boys.' As he left he pressed a card into my hand – a business card, perhaps. It was actually the card of a local restaurant, which he said was 'very good'. With a thumbs up he was off again.

The Mad Hatter made a brief appearance. This time I encountered a well-spoken, elderly man, dressed well and appropriately for his advanced years, perfectly rational, organised and polite. He was taking out a book on sleeplessness.

Startled Stewart has been away, 'abroad', but he's now back. He was coy about offering many details, but it seems that the reason he hasn't been in is that he's 'had a friend' for a while. It was going well until they had a massive argument about his new friend's lack of contributions to the rent and the friend has moved out. Startled Stewart has now resumed his routine of scurrying around town each afternoon and occasionally calling in.

Trish and her crew were in last Wednesday. As always she was wearing pink, but also sported an American baseball hat, worn backwards. She'll never change, but her world is a happy and safe place and she brings happiness with her whenever she comes in.

Brewer and Wolf have been absent for months. I assume they'll be back when the summer is over and they need the warmth of the library for their winter survival. Spencer still comes in every day to read and to use the listening post.

Joseph continues to indulge his daughter but soon she'll be at school. She teases him nowadays by hiding for as long as she dares in Fiction while he wanders around, grinning, looking for her. The last time I saw him, I caught the end of a conversation he was having with a woman who seemed eager to get away, her buggy poised at the bottom of the slope to Fiction. 'Yes, she's four now, and she's at nursery.'

'Really?'

'Yes, and . . .'

But the woman was pushing her child away.

The Travelling Man has not been in for a month. This is a bad sign. His routine was so established that it must mean there's something seriously amiss. Perhaps his travelling days are over and his daughters are now tending to him.

I saw the Thin Man yesterday. He saw me and smiled a strange smile suggesting that he knew something I didn't. Perhaps he does.

And, now among the regulars are a number of the ex-staff, now civilians. They're greeted with hugs and fondness, but soon when those who worked with them have moved on, they'll merge with the regulars.

The tannoy bing-bongs and the recorded announcement is played out. 'Can I have your attention, please? The library will close in twenty minutes. Twenty minutes. Thank you.'

I see Facilities Steph sharking round the main doors, waiting for the moment when she can begin to chivvy the stragglers out. I ask her about the sewers. The problems seem to have been resolved, but I'm intrigued to know how.

'Yeah,' she says. 'Well, the company is booked to come in every three months now and flush out the pipes. It's like the building gets an enema. Does the trick.'

'Good.'

'And the rats' tunnel has been capped off so they can't get in either.'

I leave the main desk for a quick circuit of the Periodicals table to collect the discarded newspapers, paper cups, sandwich boxes, orange peel and a number of books that people have taken from the shelves but not bothered to return. The barista in the café is closing the metal shutter on her chiller cabinet and switching off the coffee machine. There are several black bin liners of rubbish awaiting collection by the cleaners when they begin their shift the following day.

A young, attractive woman takes a seat in Periodicals and reaches down to take off her trainers. From her bag she takes out a pair of brown high-heeled shoes, which she slips on, dropping her trainers into her bag. She takes a small mirror out of her handbag and checks her face. A man, looking up from *The Times*, watches her prepare for her evening out. She sees him watching and smiles. He returns his attention hurriedly to his newspaper. The last fifteen minutes pass slowly. Those borrowing books are using the automatic machines and the desks are unvisited.

After the five-minute closure warning is played out, Sleepless Nigel makes his way to the doors with his belongings. He's been on his best behaviour for the past few weeks and has not had to be forcibly ejected at the end of the day. He waves towards the desk, and says goodnight to Steph, who is still by the door.

The final bing-bong: 'Can I have your attention, please. The library is now closed. Please make your way immediately to the exit. The library is closed.'

The recorded voice on the tannoy is a familiar one. It's only now that I realise it belongs to one of the staff who left a couple of months ago. But it's a younger version of her voice – lighter. It belongs to a time ten years before when the library, like those working in it, had a future.

On the upper and lower floors, now otherwise silent, the sound of the tills being 'kicked' and popping out from their drawers; then, from all corners of the building, the staff, bearing their money-laden till trays, make their way to the mezzanine floor to the safe in the cash office where they will be deposited and the walkie-talkies put in the chargers.

Coming out from his office to survey his empire, Trev climbs the stairs to the open mezzanine corridor, watching the final customer leave. 'Tough day?' he asks as I pass him.

'Yes. Short-staffed.'

He smiles; he knows what's going on.

'In tomorrow?'

'Friday.'

'See you then. Goodnight, young man,' he says. 'Don't do anything I wouldn't do.'

'Goodnight, Trev.'

Having collected my coat, I make my way to the back stairs and find my name, scrawled in the signing-in book. I draw a black line across the page and terminate it with '7 p.m.'. I pass the pen to the next colleague in line waiting to sign out, take the short set of stairs to the street door and leave the building by the side exit. As I walk away up the narrow street I turn back and see that the lights in the upstairs office are being switched off, one by one, as the factory is closed down for another day.

Appendix

The Dewey Decimal Classification (© Dewey services)

FIRST SUMMARY
The Ten Main Classes
000 Computer science, information & general works
100 Philosophy & psychology
200 Religion
300 Social sciences
400 Language
500 Science
600 Technology
700 Arts & recreation
800 Literature
900 History & geography

SECOND SUMMARY
The Hundred Divisions
000 Computer science, knowledge & systems
010 Bibliographies
020 Library & information sciences
030 Encyclopaedias & books of facts
040 [Unassigned]
050 Magazines, journals & serials

060 Associations, organisations & museums

070 News media, journalism & publishing

080 Quotations

090 Manuscripts & rare books

100 Philosophy

110 Metaphysics

120 Epistemology

130 Parapsychology & occultism

140 Philosophical schools of thought

150 Psychology

160 Logic

170 Ethics

180 Ancient, medieval & eastern philosophy

190 Modern western philosophy

200 Religion

210 Philosophy & theory of religion

220 The Bible

230 Christianity & Christian theology

240 Christian practice & observance

250 Christian pastoral practice & religious orders

260 Christian organisations, social work & worship

270 History of Christianity

280 Christian denominations

290 Other religions

300 Social sciences, sociology & anthropology

310 Statistics

320 Political science

330 Economics

340 Law

350 Public administration & military science

360 Social problems & social services

370 Education

380 Commerce, communications & transportation
390 Customs, etiquette & folklore
400 Language
410 Linguistics
420 English & Old English languages
430 German & related languages
440 French & related languages
450 Italian, Romanian & related languages
460 Spanish & Portuguese languages
470 Latin & Italic languages
480 Classical & modern Greek languages
490 Other languages
500 Science
510 Mathematics
520 Astronomy
530 Physics
540 Chemistry
550 Earth sciences & geology
560 Fossils & prehistoric life
570 Life sciences; biology
580 Plants (Botany)
590 Animals (Zoology)
600 Technology
610 Medicine & health
620 Engineering
630 Agriculture
640 Home & family management
650 Management & public relations
660 Chemical engineering
670 Manufacturing
680 Manufacture for specific uses
690 Building & construction

700 Arts

710 Landscaping & area planning

720 Architecture

730 Sculpture, ceramics & metalwork

740 Drawing & decorative arts

750 Painting

760 Graphic arts

770 Photography & computer art

780 Music

790 Sports, games & entertainment

800 Literature, rhetoric & criticism

810 American literature in English

820 English & Old English literatures

830 German & related literatures

840 French & related literatures

850 Italian, Romanian & related literatures

860 Spanish & Portuguese literatures

870 Latin & Italic literatures

880 Classical & modern Greek literatures

890 Other literatures

900 History

910 Geography & travel

920 Biography & genealogy

930 History of ancient world (to ca. 499)

940 History of Europe

950 History of Asia

960 History of Africa

970 History of North America

980 History of South America

990 History of other areas

The Third Summary contains a thousand further subdivisions.

Notes

1   Alberto Manguel, *The Library at Night* (New Haven and London: Yale University Press, 2006), p. 24.

2   Manguel, *The Library at Night*, p. 22.

3   Alan Bennett, 'Baffled at a Bookcase', reprinted in Rebecca Gray (ed.), *The Library Book* (London: Profile Books, 2012), p. 25.

4   Bennett, 'Baffled at a Bookcase', p. 41.

5   Ernest A. Savage, *Old English Libraries: The Making, Collection and Use of Books during the Middle Ages* (London: Methuen, 1911).

6   Matthew Battles, *Library: An Unquiet History* (London: Vintage, 2004), p. 58.

7   Wayne A. Wiegand, *Irrepressible Reformer: A Biography of Melvil Dewey* (Chicago: American Library Association, 1996), p. 44.

8   Don Borchert, *Library Confidential: Oddballs, Geeks and Gangstas in the Public Library* (London: Virgin, 2007).

9   Manguel, *The Library at Night*, p. 56.

10 Battles, *Library*, p. 79.

11 19 December 1666. Samuel Pepys, *The Diary of Samuel Pepys*, ed. Henry B. Wheatley (London: George Bell and Sons, 1899).

12 Melvil Dewey, 'Dewey Classification Beginning', *Library Journal*, no. 45 (15 February 1920), quoted in Wiegand, *Irrepressible Reformer*, p. 21.

13 Wiegand, *Irrepressible Reformer*, p. 21. The Appendix lists the ten Dewey categories, and the hundred categories of the 'Second Summary'.

14 Joshua Kendall, 'Melvil Dewey: Compulsive Innovator', *American Libraries Magazine* (24 March 2014).

15   Timothy W. Ryback, *Hitler's Private Library: The Books that Shaped His Life* (London: The Bodley Head, 2009).

16   William L. Shirer, *The Rise and Fall of the Third Reich: A History of Nazi Germany* (New York: Simon & Schuster, 1960).

17   Ryback, *Hitler's Private Library*.

18   Ryback, *Hitler's Private Library*.

19   Manguel, *The Library at Night*. The story is from Vladimir Nabokov/ Elena Sikorskaja, *Nostalgia* (Milan: Rosellina Archinto, 1989), letter dated 9 October 1945.

20   Steve Albrecht, 'Your Library Can Be a Dangerous Place', *Psychology Today* (26 March 2012), https://www.psychologytoday.com/blog/ the-act-violence/201203/your-local-library-can-be-a-dangerous-place.

21   Tomaso Montanari, 'Saccheggio dei Girolamini, nessuno è intoccabile', *Il Fatto Quotidiano* (28 August 2013), http://www. ilfattoquotidiano.it/2013/08/28/saccheggio-dei-girolamini/694655.

22   Halliwell's statement to the police, 28 April 1962, quoted in John Lahr, *Prick Up Your Ears* (London: Allen Lane, 1978), p. 95.

23   Patricia Johnson, 'Money and Mr Orton', *Evening News* (9 June 1967), quoted in Lahr, *Prick Up Your Ears*, p. 97.

24   Andrew Carnegie, *Autobiography of Andrew Carnegie* (London: Constable, 1920).

25   Carnegie, *Autobiography*.

26   Carnegie, *Autobiography*.

27   Carnegie, *Autobiography*.

28   Louisa Mellor, 'Libraries and Why I Think They Matter', *Den of Geek* (5 April 2016), http://www.denofgeek.com/books-comics/ libraries/39660/libraries-and-why-i-think-they-matter.

29   Tennessee Williams, 'The Malediction', *Vintage Williams*.

30   Bella Bathurst, 'The Secret Life of Libraries', in Gray (ed.), *The Library Book*, p. 75.

31   Ray Oldenburg, *Celebrating the Third Place* (New York: Marlowe, 2000).

32   Tom Holland, 'The Library of Babylon', in Gray (ed.), *The Library Book*.